NO MORE STUPIDTRY

NO MORE STUPIDTRY

Insights for the Modern World

LLOYD LIM

TATE PUBLISHING
AND ENTERPRISES, LLC

Published by Tate Publishing & Enterprises, LLC
127 E. Trade Center Terrace | Mustang, Oklahoma 73064 USA
1.888.361.9473 | www.tatepublishing.com

Tate Publishing is committed to excellence in the publishing industry. The company reflects the philosophy established by the founders, based on Psalm 68:11,
"The Lord gave the word and great was the company of those who published it."

Cover design by Norlan Balazo
Interior design by Richell Balansag

Published in the United States of America

ISBN: 978-1-68293-825-6
1. Social Science / Essays
2. Business & Economics / Management
16.01.28

For my mom and dad, who gave me
everything and were my best friends

Acknowledgements

My business acquaintance Calvin Hutton and my sister Susan Liang provided feedback on a draft of the manuscript. I am thankful for the political and policy banter I have engaged in over the years with Sam Thomsen, Sue Liang, Wayne C. Metcalf III, J. P. Schmidt, Andrew Brody, Harry Imster, Chris Campbell, Matt Chapman, Colin Moore, Dick Rowland, and Joe Kent. Some input on lawyers came from two with top-level integrity, Carole Richelieu and Dianne Winter Brookins. I talked about military issues with two veterans I am lucky to know, Mary Wilkowski and Eddie Quan.

I owe special thanks to my colleague Janet Eli for providing encouragement. I owe a lot to all of my teachers over the years, whose wisdom is scattered throughout this book, but particularly William Messer, Kathy Hannah Eden, Edward Tayler, Neils Ostbye, Leon Letwin, Julian Eule, Daniel Hays Lowenstein, Reginald Worthley, Jack Suyderhoud, and Robert Doktor. Of course, if I have any wisdom, it is mostly thanks to my parents, particularly my mother, Lily, who loved sayings.

About the Author

The author has worked in government and business as a lawyer and a manager. He has a particular expertise in finance and in the nexus between the government and the marketplace. He has a BA in English literature from Columbia University, a JD from UCLA, an MBA from the University of Hawaii at Manoa, and the CPCU designation. He has written three books: *Reinventing Government: A Practitioner's Guide*, *Basic Stuff That Everyone Should Know*, and *Beyond Obamacare: Solving the Healthcare Cost Problem*. He lives in Honolulu, Hawaii, and enjoys playing the piano.

Organizing Principle by Way of Quotations

Living is easy with eyes closed, misunderstanding all you see. (Beatles, "Strawberry Fields Forever")

Your eyes can deceive you, don't trust them. (Obi Wan Kenobi, *Star Wars*)

And you sit at your window when evening falls and you dream it all true. (Franz Kafka, "An Imperial Message")

You got to get your mind right, Luke. (Warden, *Cool Hand Luke*)

Contents

Preface

Why write a book? There are millions of books listed on Amazon, and tens of thousands of new titles are sold each year in the United States alone. As one of my grade school pals said, "Writing a book is pretentious." It is like a little brat who taunts you by saying, "I know something you don't know." It is disrespectful of the idea expressed in Rudyard Kipling's classic poem "If," when he says, "Yet don't look too good or talk too wise." I take these issues seriously, but I still must speak. The reason is that my view of professionals has changed greatly since I started my career a quarter century ago.

Like a lot of young people, I looked up to older people. I assumed that anyone working in a big, successful organization must know what they're doing. After some time, I learned the hard way that what people know is dwarfed by what they don't know, and that sometimes people don't know even basic things that they should be expected to know. The main reason this happens is because the world is very big and complicated, and no one can know very much of it. The other reason is that most people are too busy to read very often, or they are just plain lazy. The other reason is that there is often a cost associated with picking up new information, and some people can't afford that. The final reason is that our teachers don't always have a good sense of relevance because many of them are in academia from cradle to grave.

A few years ago, I wrote another book called *Basic Stuff That Everyone Should Know*. The idea for that book came to me because I had spent nearly twenty years talking to the public on the telephone, and I had discovered that our education system was leaving some serious gaps in knowledge. That book was an attempted remedy. In effect, it was designed to be a kind of basic job training or workforce development tool. It was designed to provide a floor of knowledge.

This new book that you are holding in your hand is based on the same idea but designed for a target audience with greater sophistication, such as someone aspiring to management, entrepreneurship, or politics. Now most business books focus on the inside of an organization. I am more interested in looking outside into the external environment. But this act of looking outward forces an examination of how we think about the world because we never really see the world for what it truly is. The world is far too complex to fit inside the human mind, and we therefore must create a construct or a model or a representation of reality. This inevitably results in an oversimplification or reduction.

About a dozen years ago, I did a piano reduction of the music from the movie *The Omen* by Jerry Goldsmith called "The New Ambassador." What I mean by a reduction is that I could not reproduce all the instruments and voices of a full orchestra, so I simplified the music to be playable by solo piano. The idea is to capture the essence of the music while leaving out a lot of the detail. In this book, I do the same kind of reduction to show you the big picture so that you don't lose the forest for the trees. You will fly like an eagle surveying the landscape instead of crawling on the dirt like a blind worm. As to the details, you can fill them in later on Google and Amazon. There is plenty of information out there. The question is whether we have given people the filters or constructs that they need to make sense of that information quickly.

Now to embark on this learning experience, the first step is to prepare your mind. I was fortunate to attend an Ivy League college, and the first day of orientation, they had a class where the teacher talked about the importance of "doubt." People have a tendency to think they know a lot, and the less experience they have, the more they tend to think that. My first boss on Wall Street truly impressed me when I asked him a question, and he said, "I just don't know." I learned well from him. Many years later, I had a call from a customer, and he asked me a question. I said, "I don't know, I don't know." He said, "Boy, are you ever a lawyer." For lawyers, knowing what one knows and can prove and what one does not know and cannot prove are crucial.

The philosopher who made this issue famous was René Descartes in the *Meditations on First Philosophy*. He said, "I think, therefore I am." Actually, that is an oversimplification. His true point was that while he could doubt that he existed, he could not doubt that he was doubting, and that, therefore, he must conclude that he existed. Doubt is the mark of the skeptic and the basic tool of critical thinking. A related bit of trivia is that a lawyer normally does not put a witness on the witness stand unless they have personal knowledge of what they are talking about or can be qualified as an expert. But everyone knows that, right? Do they?

Governor Howard Dean was on MSNBC one night talking about the movie *American Sniper* and how the people flocking to see the film were angry. What's the problem with that statement? Dean didn't see the movie, and he never met those people. Well, he went to Harvard Medical School, so he just knows things, see? The fact that our higher education system produces people who claim to know things that they cannot possibly know is part of the reason for this book.

I have sometimes been accused of being an academic or philosopher, mostly by people who want to put me in a box so that I don't threaten them. Actually, I am a practical man. I have run a small family business, I have been an administrator in government, and I have been a lawyer in the private sector and government. I have done structured finance and health insurance work, neither of which is simple. Academics are important to our system for a whole variety of reasons, and I value my friendship with the few who will deign to speak to me. But sometimes they can be too theoretical, too complex, and too narrow. One professor I heard of studies nematodes. Another studies the economics of co-ops. It isn't much wonder then that these folks don't turn into big-picture philosophers like Plato or Adam Smith. One of my favorite lines from a movie is from *Dangerous Liaisons* when Glenn Close as the Marquise de Merteuil says, "Like most intellectuals, he's intensely stupid." I don't think of myself as an academic. This book is partly modeled after the essays of Michel de Montaigne, who had a comment on academics that is worth repeating:

> But what about the things I have caught others doing? They bedeck themselves in other men's armour, with not even their fingertips showing. As it is easy for the learned to do on some commonplace subject, they carry through their projected work with bits of what was written in ancient times, patched together, higgledy-piggedly. (*The Complete Essays*, 166)

Truth to be told, this very book is a patchwork of ideas that I have come to partly because others have thought them first. I stand on the shoulders of giants, as Sir Isaac

Newton put it. But I hope that you will find in this book that the whole is greater than the sum of its parts.

My political views are not really anyone's business, but I am not party affiliated, and I try to do straight analysis. I am very passionate about the integrity of the process for making policy decisions, but I am less concerned about the outcomes of those processes. In other words, I have faith in the system, to the extent that the process itself is not corrupted. I do not do analysis of issues with an eye toward achieving a particular outcome because my experience is that this results in intellectual dishonesty almost all the time. That, in turn, destroys credibility, makes you look like a jerk, and has evil consequences.

I want to start out with some key quotes and sayings. I love sayings because they are easy to remember and they are the method my mother used to train me as a child. If actions follow ideas, as I believe that they generally do (when they are not mere rationalizations for our preexisting desires), then thinking about thinking should matter to us. In other words, my thesis is that at least some of our problems are due to wrong thinking, not merely the tussle that happens between people pursuing their own self-interest.

Here are the quotes and sayings:

1. The times, they are a changin' (Bob Dylan).
2. Dream big, but work harder than you dream (Senator Tom Daschle, paraphrasing an old saying).

3. God helps those who help themselves (old saying).
4. If you're not making mistakes, you're not doing anything (business professor).
5. A man carries himself in his hands (old saying).
6. A man's got to know his limitations (Clint Eastwood as Dirty Harry).
7. You've got to get your feet wet (old saying).
8. The best lack all conviction, but the worst are full of passionate intensity (W. B. Yeats).
9. Why do you look at the speck in your brother's eye, but don't notice the log in your own eye? (Luke 6:41).
10. The road to hell is paved with good intentions (old saying based on scripture).
11. Sometimes people want things they ought not to want (Calvin Coolidge).
12. Whom the Gods wish to destroy, they first deprive of judgment (ancient Greek saying).
13. Who said life was fair? (one of my high school English teachers).
14. Strive not to be a success, but rather to be of value (Albert Einstein).
15. Life is so unnerving for a servant who's not serving (Lumiere from *Beauty and the Beast*).

16. Whatever you are, be a good one (Abraham Lincoln).
17. The mind is everything. What you think, you become (Buddha).
18. You make your bed; you lie in it (old saying).
19. You make your own luck (old saying).
20. Hindsight is twenty-twenty (old saying).
21. In for a penny, in for a pound (old saying).
22. You can't have your cake and eat it too (old saying).
23. Fish or cut bait (old saying).
24. Pick your poison (old saying).
25. You're damned if you do and damned if you don't (old saying).
26. Try to be kind to those less strong, be respectful to the interests of others, but be prepared to get into a fight if a bully tries to push you or your friends around (Matthew P.S. Chapman).
27. Too bad all the people who know how to run the country are busy driving taxicabs and cutting hair (George Burns).
28. Practical men, who believe themselves to be quite exempt from any intellectual influences, are usually the slaves of some defunct economist (John Maynard Keynes).

29. Don't believe everything you hear (my boss on Wall Street).
30. No conversation is private (my boss on Wall Street).
31. Three may keep a secret if two of them are dead (Benjamin Franklin).
32. You are entitled to your own opinions, but you are not entitled to your own facts (Daniel Patrick Moynihan).
33. The grass is always greener on the other side of the fence (old saying).
34. Take care of your customers, and they'll take care of you. Take care of your vendors, and they'll take care of you (old sayings).
35. Buy quality (Max Lim, my father).
36. Use the right tool for the right job (Max Lim, my father).
37. Is it better to have equality at the price of poverty or well-being at the price of inequality? (Winston Churchill).
38. Government meddling with the private sector, combined with excessively loose monetary and fiscal policy, sapped confidence, investment dried up and inflation soared (*The Economist* 2015, 31, on Brazil's economy).

39. Conserve the firm foundations of our institutions (Calvin Coolidge).
40. Governing is about credibility (Lloyd Lim).
41. Play it straight (J. P. Schmidt)
42. Don't worry about the politics; just do what you think is right (Ronald Reagan).
43. Whenever you do anything, check to make sure the American flag is flying behind you (Lloyd Lim).
44. Stay above the fray (old saying).
45. Where you stand is a function of where you sit (one of my law professors).
46. You like the view from the cheap seats? (one of my bosses).
47. Follow the KISS rule, keep it simple, stupid (old saying).
48. Don't miss the forest for the trees (old saying).
49. Don't assume anything. That way, you don't make an ass of you or me (old saying).
50. Speak softly and carry a big stick (Teddy Roosevelt).
51. Speak simply and carry a big brain (Lloyd Lim).
52. He who has great power should use it lightly (Seneca).
53. A fish rots from the head down (old saying).
54. Power tends to corrupt, and absolute power corrupts absolutely (Lord Acton).

55. All other things being equal, the simplest explanation is usually the best (Ockham's Razor—paraphrased, also applies to solutions).

56. As institutions influence behavior and incentives in real life, they forge the success or failure of nations. Individual talent matters at every level of society, but even that needs an institutional framework to transform it into a positive force (Daron Acemoglu and James A. Robinson, *Why Nations Fail*, 43).

57. Culture matters too. The way that people organize institutions, define social networks, and classify the world has a crucial impact on how the government, business, and economy function (or sometimes do not function) (Gillian Tett, *The Silo Effect: the Peril of Expertise and the Promise of Breaking Down Barriers,* xii).

58. But humans in any society tend to assume that their own culture is natural. Our own social rules and classification systems we use to organize our worlds and minds are not inevitable; they are usually a function of nurture not nature (Gillian Tett, *The Silo Effect: the Peril of Expertise and the Promise of Breaking Down Barriers*, 251).

59. Culture, then, is a pool of technological and social innovations that people accumulate to help them live their lives, not a collection of arbitrary roles and

symbols that happen to befall them. (Steven Pinker, *The Blank Slate: The Modern Denial of Human Nature*, 65).

60. The striking difference between the long-term histories of people of the different continents have been due not to innate differences in the people themselves but to differences in their environments (Jared Diamond, *Guns, Germs and Steel: the Fates of Human Societies*, 389).
61. We're all in the same boat (old saying).
62. As America goes, so we go (Max S.H. Lim, my father).
63. Live and let live (old saying).
64. Nor I, nor any man that but man is, with nothing shall be pleased till he be eased with being nothing (Shakespeare, *Richard II*).
65. For those of you who want to be rich and famous, try rich first and see if that doesn't do it for you (Bill Murray).
66. Anything that can go wrong, will, and at the worst possible moment (Murphy's law).
67. What goes around comes around (old saying).
68. You reap what you sow (old saying, derived from the Bible).

69. He who has the gold makes the rules (corrupted Golden Rule).
70. Do unto others as you would have them do unto you (real Golden Rule, derived from scripture [see Matthew 7:12]). (Note that there is a variant that I believe is closer to what is in the Torah, which says that you should not do unto others as you would not have them do unto you. Interesting difference because it is less activist.)

This list of sayings could solve a lot of our problems if people would only follow them. But to truly reengineer our thinking, we must go further and deeper. We must probe the logic of our rationales, premises, and assumptions. For that hopefully exciting exercise, please read on.

Leadership and Management

I have written before on the topic of leadership in my book *Basic Stuff That Everyone Should Know*. I want to take a second crack at it and try to do a better job. The key to leadership is character and ethics. There have been some dirty, rotten scoundrels who have been leaders, but you will notice that they have also often wielded dictatorial powers. In the usual situation that we find in the workplace today, most of the people working under a leader have a choice about whether to stay or go. That is why character and ethics matter. As former Speaker of the House John Boehner has said, "If you're leading and no one is following, you're just out for a walk." William Deresiewicz put it nicely, "Leadership meant duty, honor, courage, toughness, graciousness, selflessness" (*Excellent Sheep: the Miseducation of the American Elite and the Way to a Meaningful Life* 2014, 135). To put it another way, a leader makes sure that he or she is always sending the right message to others about the kind of person that they are. According to management gurus Peter F. Drucker and Simon Sinek, a leader must inspire trust.

A leader must also have foresight, both to avoid trouble and to plan ahead for implementation. If you lead your team into a minefield, they are not going to want to stay with you. Of course, it takes a certain amount of experience and knowledge to have foresight, but some people are just better at it than others, and we don't know exactly why. Studies show that experts are no better at predicting the future than laypersons. Nassim Nicholas Taleb, in *The Black Swan*, said that anyone who thinks that they can predict the future is kidding themselves because you cannot anticipate rare, random events that have big consequences.

The problem is that anyone in leadership must guess at the future because there is no way to do the job without trying to anticipate how people are going to react to the things that you do. It may not be efficient to plan for everything when most of those things will never come to pass, but it is foolish to merely react to events because you will lose any ability you might otherwise have to shape the course of those events. You might be surprised at how many people run off and do things before they even figure out what they are doing. You might be surprised how many people advocate for ideas that they haven't even begun to think through. That's not a good way to be if you aspire to leadership.

When you're a leader, you have to be yourself and be consistent because people don't like phonies. In addition, you should try to maintain your credibility by being right. These matters may sound like they are about character, but not necessarily. These are choices; these are policies. I read my first management book in the ninth grade by Paul Hersey and Ken Blanchard called *The Management of Organizational Behavior*. I was the class president, and the principal of my high school had a PhD in leadership, and he gave me that book to read. Their basic idea is that a manager needs to change up his behavior when dealing with different people and even the same people at different times. Different strokes for the same folks is the idea in a nutshell. Great idea—except that if you turn yourself into this kind of chameleon, I think people will just see you as two-faced. So much for theory.

Woody Allen said that "90 percent of life is just showing up." Leadership is like that. You have to show face. You have to fly the flag. You have to represent your staff in communications with outside parties, and you have to stand up for them. You have to keep an eye on the external environment, and you need to understand the difference between your culture and the various cultures of the world that you are operating in. Too often, we in the United States are ethnocentric, and our misunderstandings of others cause problems. One of the dangers of our computers is that we begin to look for the world inside a machine rather than outside in the world where we can walk around and talk to people. In addition, if birds of the same feather flock together, then we should try to get out of the office now and meet new people with different viewpoints.

A leader must be decisive. Sometimes it is tempting to try to have things both ways, to split the baby, to have one's cake and eat it too. The problem is that this approach can get you into big trouble because it won't work forever. For example, polling indicates that the public wants government to provide more benefits and services at the same time that they also want lower taxes. Sorry, but that is a road to nowhere. Napoleon said that half measures lose all in war. Well, not just in war. If you want to be effective, you have to decide and go all in with the right level of commitment and resources. If you don't back up your decision with follow through, you didn't really make the decision.

Now that said, historian Paul Johnson has pointed out that you have to watch out for people who like to make decisions. People like that enjoy power and have a hungry ego. Decisions usually require information, but not all questions have answers, at least not in the short term. And you don't want to waste time collecting information that you're not going to use . That seems obvious, but I have seen many people do that sort of thing. There is always some uncertainty and ambiguity when you are going forward into the future.

There are different ways of seeing your role as a leader. You can see yourself as the king, a father, a coach, a teacher, or a vendor of services. I use the vendor approach, but you needn't. But you should have some vision of the role you play and the responsibilities you have to your staff. If your staff starts to see you as someone who is only out to glorify yourself or protect your own hide, your capacity to lead will fade rapidly.

Management is different from leadership. A manager is a glorified administrative assistant. A leader is someone for whom you would die on Pork Chop Hill. Many books have been written about management, and a lot of baloney has been sold to the public. In a way, this entire book is a book about management because I am trying to help the reader think through the kind of issues that a sophisticated manager must understand. But there is one key management issue that has to be highlighted because it is the most important.

In the movie *Star Wars*, Princess Leia says to the Grand Moff Tarkin, "The more you tighten your grip, Tarkin, the more star systems will slip through your fingers." For those who think George Lucas is silly, this is a restatement of a business school principle called the paradox of control. That principle is that the more you try to control people, the less control you have over them. To put it another way, there is always the question of whether a manager should lay hands on and direct things closely or do them himself versus delegating to others while retaining a review power. It depends on the situation and person you are dealing with, but it is also important to realize that this is often not a question of balance but that you must make a decision and choose a course of action. You cannot have your cake and eat it too because if you do that, you will send mixed messages and confuse your staff.

As with all things, having a general policy of delegation versus one of micromanagement results in different trade-offs. But the big problem with micromanagement is not only that people hate it but that you really have to know what you are doing, and most managers do not. This is why we often talk about management by objective. We tell people the goal and don't get too involved in the question of how they get there. No manager can think of everything, and you often need the help of your staff. If they hang back and just follow orders, it can turn into a great way of sabotaging you. Ideally, you empower the staff to do things without being told. Of course, the ability to avoid micromanagement depends partly on the ability of your staff. If they are very good at what they do, then less micromanagement will be needed. Also note that when you pay people more, they usually become easier to manage. If a boss is mean, abusive, and critical to the staff, obviously that will tend to lower their internal motivation. Another key part of management is knowing what people don't know and making sure that you get them the necessary information.

Now, since I am a lawyer, let me talk a bit about orders and the legal issues they raise at the risk of getting into the weeds. When you give orders, you need to say clearly what results or objectives you want to achieve, but you don't necessarily want to specify the means or tactics of how the staff arrives there. Also, after you give an order, you don't want to impede the staff by putting barriers around them or by failing to give them adequate information or tools to get the job done because that might start to look like interference or even sabotage. Although managers often have good intentions, they do not always understand the kind of spin a nasty plaintiff's lawyer could put on them. Obsessive-compulsive disorder may be good for the quality of your own work, but it can be very bad as a management technique. Think about the movie *Mommie Dearest*. In addition, if you get into a labor dispute with an employee, it is better not to rule off the top of your head. It is better to listen, think about a response, and then respond. That way, even if you don't get the substance right, you can defend the procedure and avoid looking arbitrary and capricious, which is the typical standard for abuse of discretion.

Another issue is time. Sometimes it is good to wait to deal with a problem either because you need more information, you can't figure out a solution right away, or because the problem might solve itself with the passage of time. Also, it is a good idea to sketch out the critical path because some things will take longer than others; and if they do, then they need to be front-loaded even if they might seem to belong to a later stage in the plan. In other words, the old saying "First things first" is not always true. Government management is a special case because the slowness and complexity of the bureaucratic process means that when you do implementation, you need to plan ahead by at least six months to a year.

The key issue is whether you can hire the right people for the right job. This is never easy because it is hard to find good people, and it is near impossible to find someone with exactly the right background. Those who remember the old television series *Mission: Impossible* will remember that at the start of every show, Mr. Phelps, played by Peter Graves, would sit near a table and look through a series of photos of possible IMF agents and then pick those whom he wanted to use for that week's mission. I enjoyed that part very much. It was fun to find out whether he would pick Lesley Ann Warren or Barbara Bain. But this, in a nutshell, is the key to management. You need to put together the right team and then more or less cut them loose to do their jobs. In other words, if you have competent staff, please get out of their way. Everyone is a mixed bag with certain strengths and weaknesses, and the team must be able to work together. It's not just a question of finding a bunch of rock stars and throwing them together. It's a mission for Mr. Phelps, should you decide to accept it.

In my books *Reinventing Government: A Practitioner's Guide* and *Basic Stuff That Everyone Should Know*, I talked about the difference between business and government. I am going to address that issue in a more summary fashion later, but at this juncture, what I want to say is that the key difference between a manager in business and a manager in government is that a businessperson won't waste time on nonproductive activity whereas some government managers like to create busywork or will pursue projects beyond the point where they should be terminated.

As a manager, don't be a diligent moron. Understand the difference between big and small. Keep perspective on the big picture and the long run. Don't take things too seriously, particularly yourself. Recognize that all organizations have some downtime and that downtime can be useful for creative people. Accept the fact that all people are a mixed bag and will never be perfect. Know that you are not perfect either. Recognize that while money is an important incentive, it is not the only incentive—and depending on the person, it may not be the most important consideration. Most people like to feel good about what they are doing, and the conditions under which they work matter to them. That is why managers who like to blame their staff and criticize people to make themselves feel good end up destroying morale.

A manager must correctly locate, define, and diagnose problems; determine the causes; and find a solution. If you don't do this right, you can waste a lot of time. For this exercise to work, listening is required. If a problem cannot be solved, you should try to determine that quickly so you avoid wasting resources on a futile gesture.

When writing about people, it is important to be accurate in your statements. A danger area is accusations of wrongdoing because those can be hard to prove, and we have a presumption of innocence. A lot depends on how you word things. If you simply say that the situation raises an issue of malfeasance, it is very different from a flat-out accusation. Legally, questions are not the same as conclusions. Also, you can sometimes word opinions carefully to make them look more factual, for example, by adding qualifiers. If I want to criticize someone, I try to avoid conclusions and simply recount things they said or did and let the facts speak for themselves.

Finally, a word or two on motivation. Daniel Pink's book *Drive: The Surprising Truth About What Motivates Us* (2009) is a fairly up-to-date summary of current knowledge. At page 3, in describing an experiment, he makes the key point, "The joy of the task was its own reward." Workers can have a good time if they enjoy what they are doing. But how can they enjoy what they are doing unless they are proficient at it? I have always believed that a person would not be successful if they didn't like what they were doing, but it is an overstatement. Because if you do something a long time and get good at it, you might end up enjoying it. You become the work, as one of my bosses once said. I will say more about this idea of enjoying work in a future essay, and not all of it is positive.

Now, that is a fairly short discussion compared to what is in many other books on leadership and management. The reason is that I am very skeptical that we can use a bunch of rules to manage. I don't think so. You have to be willing to respond to the situation at hand. Ideological rigidity is your enemy when dealing with people. Look at the facts of the case.

Reading and Writing

Reading and writing are basic skills that we need throughout life. Modern thinking about the brain is that it has something called plasticity, which means that it can develop and change to some extent over time. Of course, the most significant development occurs in early childhood, and the main period of development continues until about age twenty. But I myself know that some development can occur after that because my skills at reading, writing, and playing the piano have changed over time. This change did not happen fast, but about the time I turned fifty, my brain really started to fire on all cylinders. I developed fluency.

It is my view that the only way this fluency can develop is through a lot of repetition. If you want to get better at reading and writing, you have to do a lot of it. Speed-reading happens because you become able to scan around the page and cherry-pick useful information points instead of reading everything left to right inch by inch. Similarly, in music, once we learn music theory, we can easily see clusters of notes, and it no longer becomes necessary to read every notehead.

In addition, in reading books, if I already know a lot about a given topic, I can skim similar knowledge because it is not really new knowledge. Also, what happens often with nonfiction is that there may be a small part that is theoretical narrative, like what I am writing now, which is then followed by cases, examples, or anecdotes. The thing about these fact-intensive stories is that they don't really prove anything from a scientific perspective. You can't prove a general theory by citing a couple of cases. So if I am in a hurry, quite often I will just skim detailed factual material. It is an irresponsible way to read, but like everyone else, I don't have an unlimited amount of time for this kind of thing. You may ask, How can a professional do this? Answer: if you need to do a closer, more careful read, you can always read the material again. I'm talking about how you do a first pass.

There is a question about a choice between reading fiction or nonfiction; and within the nonfiction genre, between textbooks and original text, known in German as urtext. Fiction allows you to see inside people's psychology in a way that nonfiction often does not, but the danger is that you are dealing with a mixture of lies and truth, and one can get confused. The problem with my telling someone about something fictional is that it didn't really happen, so while it may be illustrative of something true about human nature, it is not actually true.

In the Renaissance, Sir Philip Sidney wrote a book called *An Apology for Poetry*. This might be translated into current English as "a defense of fiction." Sidney's thesis is that fiction is better than history or philosophy because it combines the specific facts that you find in history with the general precepts that you find in philosophy to produce a hybrid form that teaches the reader something important. Sidney is drawing from the golden mean of Aristotle, but I can confirm his point as a practical matter. The few times that I have written fiction, I have needed a theme to organize the story. As to nonfiction, textbooks provide a good overview of an entire subject, but they tend to be written for the college level and are not the most difficult things to read, so they do not test you, or develop you, completely.

Original text is sometimes difficult to read, but it gives you a good flavor of the way the writer's mind works, which you cannot get from a textbook. For example, I learned from reading Adam Smith and John Maynard Keynes in the original that Smith is empirical in his thinking and that Keynes is a theoretician. Some philosophers, but not all, believe that language is thinking and that this is how our view of the world is determined. I think that there are other factors and that some people think in other ways, such as visually. But there is no doubt that language plays an important role in how we think. For example, I have often wondered whether the German language had an influence on the ability of composers like Bach, Mozart, and Beethoven (among others) to write excellent classical music. I can't prove it, but I strongly suspect that there is a connection.

Now, I don't claim to be the greatest writer in history. That prize goes to William Shakespeare. But I think I am competent. If I were teaching writing to kids, I would give them one rule, which is Strunk & White's rule number 17: "Omit needless words." Actually, this is not a new idea. Ecclesiastes 5:3 says in relevant part, "And a fool's voice is known by multitude of words." Similarly, Shakespeare said in *Hamlet*, "Brevity is the soul of wit." Two good writing exercises are the précis, where you take a piece of writing and shorten it by a specified percentage of words without loss of meaning; and the executive summary, which is a one-page brief to the decision-maker who sits on top of a longer explanatory memorandum. In each case, the student's goal is to be concise.

There are many examples of concise writing, but two of my favorites are set forth below:

The First Amendment to the US Constitution (in the Bill of Rights), which reads,

> Congress shall make no law respecting an establishment of religion, or prohibiting the free exercise thereof, or abridging the freedom of speech, or of the press, or the right of the people peaceably to assemble, and to petition the Government for a redress of grievances.

The second inaugural at the state legislature of Calvin Coolidge, which reads,

> Conserve the firm foundations of our institutions. Do your work with the spirit of a soldier in the public service. Be loyal to the Commonwealth, and to yourselves. And be brief—above all things, be brief.

Some people have said that when you hire people, you should look at a writing sample because clear writing reflects clear thinking. Well, behavior and ethics are more important to me when hiring, but it is always helpful if someone can demonstrate on-target, focused, logical thinking by writing a clear and concise sentence.

I want to do a riff on the story of Adam and Eve from Genesis. First, I would argue that Genesis is allegorical, not literal. Some evangelicals in America started the trend toward the view that the Bible is literally true in the mid-nineteenth century, but that view is not universally held by all Christians everywhere. I think Genesis is mostly about who we are as human beings—that is, who we are inside ourselves and in relation to the external world and God. Genesis 3:19 is a particularly interesting read:

> And out of the ground the Lord God formed every beast of the field, and every fowl of the air; and brought them unto Ad'am to see what he would call them: and whatsoever Ad'am called every living creature, that was the name thereof.

The power to name the animals is the power of classification by language. It is the power to determine the relationship between a word and a thing. This may seem to be a simple matter, but let us remember that the thing is usually an object outside ourselves, and the name is inside our heads. This, then, is the key method by which we develop constructs about the world as I discussed in the Preface. The ability to divide up the world into things with names is an abstract tool that gives us power over those things.

A good example of this comes from the time of manifest destiny in US history, when the white settlers pushed out the indigenous population of Native Americans. People have talked about the role of superior technology, exotic germs, racism, and genocidal behavior in this process; but they overlook the fact that when a culture with property rights goes up against a culture without property rights, the latter loses. The reason is that with property rights comes the market system, and no one can stand against that for long. The rule of law is based on language. Powerful stuff. The pen is mightier than the sword.

Another key moment from literature is the line from Shakespeare's play *Romeo and Juliet*, where Shakespeare poses the issue "What's in a name?" and answers that "a rose by any other name would smell as sweet." Shakespeare is saying that the names *Capulet* or *Montague* are just words and have nothing to do with the real world. Of course, that is not the ultimate message of the play. Romeo and Juliet die because society attaches importance to their family names, and society has power. Shakespeare is making the sociological observation that words derive meaning from the social context. In other words, this is not just a lot of clever rhyming. Shakespeare is a sophisticated thinker, and this was long before the social sciences were created.

One final thing to consider is the difference between an oral tradition and a written tradition. Of course, writing things down allows for a much broader dispersion of the information and an elimination of the problem of distortion of the message through repetition. It also allows us to remember complex and lengthy narratives without being forced to have the prodigious memory of a Homer. But most important is the fact that with writing, a person can compare conflicting information and ideas. We can compare Plato to Aristotle, and in reconciling the conflict is borne some part of our critical thinking. But I am getting a bit ahead of myself and bleeding into the next essay.

If you are doing some substantial writing, I think it is a good idea to sketch out the ideas and issues you want to cover before sitting down at the Word processor. I use a combination of spiral notebooks or three-ring binders and 3 × 5 index cards to jot down my notes. The good thing about index cards is that it is easy to rearrange the order. I got that idea from screenwriter Lawrence Kasdan. The idea is to take the reader on a tour of your thinking, so if the tour is arranged logically, it can help a lot.

We live in an information economy, and most of us today are not, say, welders but knowledge workers. In the 1970s, there was a Sidney Pollack film called *Three Days of the Condor* with Robert Redford and Faye Dunaway. At one point, the CIA guys are talking about Redford and trying to figure out who he is. John Houseman says, "Tell me about Condor." The other guy says, "He reads"—there is an interruption—"he reads everything." One guy doesn't get it, but Houseman says, "Yes, very good." Condor was a new kind of hero, essentially a giant nerd who could beat people with superior knowledge. That describes well today's game, and you take a risk if you don't play it. If you don't read, what is going to be in your head? You are what you eat. You can't be competent in most areas without doing some reading. And by the way, for those of you who might call me a snob, I know how to weld also.

Fact versus Opinion

One of my favorite sayings is Daniel Patrick Moynihan's classic: "You are entitled to your own opinions, but you are not entitled to your own facts." The point is that lying can only really pertain to facts and not to opinions. But upon closer examination, we can see that the line between fact and opinion is not always completely clear.

Presumably, a fact can either be proven true or false; but if we think about how we know things, there are varying degrees of certainty around this question. As Nassim Nicholas Taleb pointed out in his book *The Black Swan*, people once believed there were no such things as black swans until they were discovered in Australia. Of course, we all know that many people once believed the Earth to be flat, although we now know it is not, at least when viewed from a distance. These are just examples of the untrustworthiness of some facts. You cannot really falsify an opinion because it is usually a preference, such as "I like Bach more than Beethoven." The other thing to notice about opinions is that when taking positions on policy issues, you can say that someone is dead wrong only if they are wrong factually. If someonc is making a choice based on an opinion about a preference for one set of consequences over another, you cannot really say that they are dead wrong, only that you disagree with them.

Henry Kissinger makes an important point about facts in his book *World Order* (2015) on page 350. He says, "Facts are rarely self-explanatory; their significance, analysis, and interpretation—at least in the foreign policy world—depend on context and relevance." To put it more simply, there is often some subjectivity in dealing with facts because we see through our own personal prisms and paradigms. Or as the ancient Greek skeptics put it, "All is opinion." Of course, that goes a bit too far. If a bullet goes through your forehead, that is not a matter of opinion. But you get the point. Humans can distort information.

One question is, Am I lying if I present cherry-picked facts and omit some other facts? That is debatable. Under securities law standards, you can be held liable for an omission if the statement needed the omitted fact in order to avoid being misleading. But under most insurance law standards, the insurer need only avoid saying something misleading. I prefer the idea that one should tell the truth, the whole truth, and nothing but the truth. However, as a lawyer, I can tell you that one-sided argumentation is our daily bread because our assumption is that the decision-maker will compare notes between the parties and sort out the truth. If the person weighing the two sides is smart enough, maybe this works; but if not, then it doesn't. One of the problems with this adversarial approach is that if someone lies and this lie is not corrected by the process and ends up in the decision-maker's head, you could argue that the process itself has been subverted and that the decision that results is not truly valid. Since process matters a lot in a democratic system, lies should be considered anathema to the formulation of public policy.

Another question is, Am I lying if I believe what I am saying? Christianity would absolve you ethically, but there is still the problem of other people relying on your misstatement to their detriment. I think part of the question is whether you have done reasonable diligence to find the truth. People who lie because they are mistaken but who act with reckless disregard for the truth or falsity of a statement could be considered culpable even if they did not lie intentionally.

There are many different types of bias, as a good course or book on critical thinking would show; but for me, the most important are observation bias, recall bias, and confirmation bias. Observation bias simply means that things depend on your point of view. If you look at a clock from the front and then from the side, it doesn't look the same at all. Recall bias simply means that we forget a lot of facts, and in remembering, we overemphasize some facts over others. Confirmation bias simply means that if we already hold a view of something, we tend to seek out facts that further confirm our preexisting beliefs and discount facts that contradict them. In other words, even if we think we are dealing with facts, we are cherry-picking.

One also needs to be careful about the use of analogies because the more you drill down into an analogy, the less accurate it seems to be. Rarely are analogies on all fours, as it were. We may think in analogies, we may learn by analogies, we may lawyer by analogy, but there is a lack of precision to the thought process involved that we should be mindful of. Those people who keep saying that this or that is like Nazi Germany don't have a clue what they are talking about. Perhaps the most crucial bit of critical thinking is the notion that just because two variables (phenomena) are correlated does not mean that one causes the other. Pope Francis has complained that capitalism causes poverty, but poverty existed long before capitalism and was more pervasive. Just because it rains when I walk outside doesn't mean that one caused the other. Probably the best way to foster critical thinking is by reading broadly across many subject areas and on both sides of the political spectrum. Use multiple sources.

A deeper question is whether the truth always matters. Of course, if you are making decisions based on a false vision of the way the world works, then your actions or plans or policies might not work. We might end up saying,

"That dog won't hunt." But if you believe in something that is not true, and that belief causes you to behave in a good and beneficial way, then perhaps it is okay to believe in it. For example, soldiers going into battle where they might die might have their courage bolstered by an untrue feeling that they are not going to be the ones to die today. My mother told me that little white lies are okay. I'm not sure about that, but it is an issue to be considered. Of course, if you are a guy and your wife or girlfriend asks, "Do I look fat?" you may want to say no. At least, I think that is the case. Or at least don't say, "You're weighing in at gross tonnage."

The fact is that people will lie if they have to, and unfortunately, given the legal liability and the partisanship we see today, they often have to lie if they have gotten themselves into a bad position. So the key is to avoid getting yourself into a position where you will have to lie. In other words, you have to think ahead. Sometimes people feel that if they are good family people and religious, they are not going to get into trouble. It doesn't work that way. Even relatively nice people can get in trouble sometimes.

This may seem to be an odd place for it, but I want to discuss humor. I love humor, and I use it all the time, despite the fact that I skate dangerously close to Title VII violations pretty regularly. I'm not politically correct because I do satire. My tone of voice and mannerisms when I deliver these comments suggest that I am making a joke, but if someone put this stuff into a written transcript, it might not look funny to some people. But on to my main point. A famous comedian once said that humor is a violation of social norms. I agree with that. What he is saying is that it is inherent in most humor to be at least slightly offensive.

In the movie *The Untouchables*, Al Capone (played by Robert De Niro) says, "We laugh because it's funny, and we laugh because it's true." If a joke is offensive but true, people may laugh. If it offensive but not true, they may not. They may get mad. Because humor is difficult to calibrate for everyone who is listening, you always run a risk when you tell a joke that someone isn't going to like it. Some people can't handle being made fun of for a whole variety of reasons. For example, if you have been victimized by someone in the past or endured hardship, it can oversensitize you to certain issues. My own view is that despite the risk of hurting someone's feelings, I would not like to live in a world without humor. Someone once said that the more intelligent people find almost everything to be very funny. In my experience, that is often true.

Of course, some jokes are not about truth but are more nonsense jokes. One of my favorites in this genre from grade school is this: "Do you know what baja is? The sound of laughing sheep. What is sisboombah? The sound of exploding sheep. Ssss-boom-baaaa!" There is a visual thing you can do with your hands when you say the punch line that makes it even funnier.

Finally, I must end this essay with the famous quote from Donald Rumsfeld about critical thinking. He said, "There are known knowns. There are things we know that we know. There are known unknowns. That is to say, there are things that we now know we don't know. But there are also unknown knowns. There are things we do not know we don't know." Rumsfeld may not be the nicest guy in the world, but he had a distinguished public service career, including being a Navy pilot. And he went to Princeton on a partial scholarship, so I doubt that we can say that he is stupid.

Critical Thinking, Science, and Religion

As I discussed earlier, critical thinking boils down to doubt and knowing what you know and what you don't know. Part of the critical-thinking training comes from comparing two writings that contradict each other. Another part comes from experience and testing your theories, constructs, and expectations against the reality of the world. The second kind of critical thinking takes a lifetime to develop; and of course, as reality changes over time, your theories and constructs must keep up. Our thinking as humans has always been somewhat empirical in that we must test things out against the world to see if they work. We learn the hard way. If a caveman used the wrong weapon against a saber-toothed tiger, he might not survive the encounter. Sir Francis Bacon was a great Renaissance thinker who laid a foundation for the scientific method in *The New Organon*. His aphorism 1 states,

Man, being the servant and interpreter of Nature, can do and understand so much and so much only as he has observed in fact or in thought of the course of nature: Beyond this he neither knows anything nor can do anything.

This is a far cry from Plato's *The Republic*, which posited that truth could be derived in the abstract from the "forms."

One of the flaws of our education system is that we teach children that science necessarily means truth. Well, it depends on how you define *science*. We know that applied science or technology must be true in the sense that if a device didn't work, then we couldn't sell it to people. But as to the more theoretical sciences, like quantum mechanics or climate change, testing can be difficult. There is a debate about what the exact parameters of science are. Some think that it is a matter of creating a theory and proving it through repeatable experiments or, more precisely, proving that the theory cannot be falsified. Some think that correlation analyses that do not prove causation are not really science. Some think that any science must have a standard unit of measure.

Now, we must recognize that some systems are too big and complex and too variable to subject to repeatable experiments (the same point was made by Jared Diamond in *Guns, Germs, and Steel: the Fates of Human Societies* in page 407). That is why it can be difficult to call economics a science. For example, if I try to determine what mix of government and market system is the best, it can be very complicated to try to do that. In addition, since cultures differ, the results that we would get from any experiments might not produce an apples-to-apples comparison.

We should also consider the question of meta-analysis: can one compare many different studies conducted under different circumstances? The answer is that it is not easy. My experience in this from the medical field has told me that medical studies are like judicial decisions: there are some pros and some cons. You can put a whole pile of academic papers about studies on your desk, but you usually cannot add the data from different studies together because they are not done in the same way under the same conditions.

To put it simply, science is not black-and-white, and people who talk about settled science are sometimes misguided, at least in some situations. People who claim that science proves that there is no God misunderstand the situation. Science cannot prove the existence of God because the supernatural is, by definition, outside of science. Science cannot prove the existence of God, but it cannot disprove it either. Christianity understands this very well. If God's existence could be proven, then there would be no role for the leap of faith required to believe in God, Jesus Christ, and the Resurrection. It would make faith meaningless.

To use a commonplace example, in the movie *Patriot Games*, Jack Ryan (played by Harrison Ford) is asked whether anything in life is really certain. He says, "My daughter's love." Science could not prove that love, but that doesn't mean it does not exist. For this reason, I suggest that atheism is a belief or at least an ideology and that one should therefore hedge one's bets and continue to be God-fearing. In my experience as someone who came to faith gradually over a long period, it is a paradigm shift. A nonbeliever sees God nowhere. A believer sees God in everything. Or as Shakespeare put it in *Hamlet*, "There is Providence in the fall of a sparrow." That doesn't mean you should start praying for parking spaces because the degree of God's intervention in earthly affairs can be debated. It just means that being grateful and thanking God every now and then is a good way of hedging your bets. The philosopher Blaise Pascal recommended that sort of hedging a long time ago. Life can be hard, but it is harder for some than for others. If you have ever seen how a quadriplegic lives or how hard it can be for a parent to care for a badly disabled child, then you will know that many of you, like me, are just darn lucky as things are. The United States is a wealthy, technologically advanced country. Our first-world problems are different from third-world problems.

Karl Marx thought religion was the opiate of the masses. Sigmund Freud thought religion was a childhood neurosis. I can't be sure about all of that, but I do know that we cannot expect government and law enforcement to handle all bad behavior because we simply don't have the resources. Voluntary compliance matters. In addition, only a few laws are really about morality. Law is more often about policy.

If religion helps society control bad behavior through self-control, then we might not want to throw the baby out with the bathwater as some advocate. Thus, even if Karl Marx was right that religion was the opiate of the masses, maybe it serves a useful purpose. We shall see, as time passes and society becomes more secular, whether everything holds together. Most of the great philosophers believed that a moral system needed some kind of enforcement, such as punishment in hell, and some kind of absolute standard, like God. My own view is that a belief in God helps me accept what I cannot change or control. If that is palliative, so be it.

Do atheists have an answer to the question of how we get people to accept the system and the power plays and mistakes that happen every day that can hurt them? If so, I haven't heard what it is. To me, we do not really know what happens with the passage of time. As we get further and further away from generations that were deeply religious, will we remain a moral society? I think that because my paternal grandfather was a minister, our family has these instincts despite the fact that my parents didn't force religion upon us. But what happens three or four generations down the road? Another clever social experiment. Watch out for that stuff.

I want to talk about evil. St. Augustine thought evil was privation or distance from God. The Manicheans thought that there was an ongoing battle between good and evil.

Augustine actually started out as a Manichean, but he later shifted his views because he did not want to posit evil as an affirmative entity or force opposing God, given his belief that God is all-powerful. Some modern thinkers believe that evil is a lack of empathy. I think part of evil is simply that it is easy to do bad things to others because it doesn't affect you and you don't feel the consequences. Or I could go further and say that there is an ego gratification and even a sexual component to power. I would also say, however, that people who need to use power to feel good may have feelings of a lack of power and control that they are compensating for.

In addition, some people who used to be seen as evil could probably be classified today as having a serious mental illness. Atheists sometimes think Christianity is foolish because it does not account for the evil that men do; but they don't realize that Christian doctrine assumes that human beings have free will and that, therefore, you can't blame everything on God. The problem of how you reconcile evil with the idea of an all-powerful benevolent deity is the problem of theodicy, and you can Google it.

My own view—and I may be a doctrinal heretic for saying this—is that when people go too far in their evil and sadism, like the Nazis, we do not have to apply general Christian principles such as forgiveness or turning the other cheek. I believe that the assumption behind those principles is that you are dealing with people who are somewhat like yourself and who are therefore entitled to be cut some slack. Although we may all be capable of becoming Nazis, many of us are so far away from that, that it does not apply. That said, we need to recognize that goodness is, in part, a luxury item. If the basic human needs aren't met, then bad behavior is almost inevitable. In other words, sometimes evil has something to do with the situation one finds oneself in. Not to absolve adults of personal responsibility, you understand. If you're weak and cowardly and either do evil or stand by while evil is being done, then you may be held to account for that.

I think we also have to consider the extent to which lying also results in evil or is evil in and of itself. I'm not sure about that, but it is worth thinking about. Another interesting question is, Do people who are evil know that they are? I think some of them do not know. I think people can rationalize their own selfishness easily, and some people think that the ends justify the means. Also, if you do not oppose evil because you are trying to keep your job in order to feed your children, is that really culpable behavior? Hannah Arendt talked about the banality of evil, and there is something to that.

I have always been a bit skeptical about the attempt by psychology to pathologize human behavior. I don't mind a system of classification. I don't mind research. I don't mind pathologizing very serious aberrant behavior. But I am skeptical about mislabeling behavior that is well within the range of normal and that a significant number of people exhibit as a pathology, whether it is narcissism or sociopathology or whatever. Sometimes you have to be a narcissist. Sometimes you have to be a sociopath. It doesn't mean that you should be locked up in the rubber room. It depends on your job and the situation at hand. Maybe we should think of diversity as meaning that everyone has a role to play. For example, do you want to send the Presbyterian minister and television personality Fred Rogers to kill terrorists? Anyway, back to the original point, I heard a psychologist on the evening news in Hawaii claim that there was something called *hurricane fatigue syndrome* just because we had a number of recent close calls. I think that is clearly pseudoscientific nonsense. Psychobabble. Of course the worst thing about pathologizing human behavior is that it tends to diminishes personal responsibility.

One final word about science: some things are just not scientific. Teaching is not a science. Parenting is not a science. Marriage is not a science. So let us not look for love in all the wrong places, as it were. Some things are just not susceptible to that kind of inquiry. Of course, people like to dress things up as science in order to give themselves credibility. A related point is the use of numbers to trick people into thinking that science is involved. A CPA I was working with once gave me a projection with a number with two decimal places. I said, "That makes you look more certain than you are about your prediction." He liked that comment. The more precise your number, the more imperative it is to state a confidence interval or a margin of error. Otherwise, you are implying a level of accuracy and certainty that does not exist, and it is misleading. If I am not certain, then I would rather state a range than a single number.

Now, there is always uncertainty; and as my astronomy professor said, "There is much certainty within uncertainty." We don't just have to go around saying, "I don't know, I don't know" all day long. But let's not try to kid each other about the level of precision associated with things like statistical modeling or regression analysis. And as the old saying goes, "Garbage in, garbage out." Most problems in statistics are about data quality. We should also remember in looking at any given number that there is a methodology behind how it was derived, and if we do not know this methodology, then we cannot fully understand what the number means. The two old jokes along these lines are, "Statistics don't lie, statisticians do" and, "There are lies, damned lies, and statistics."

What Is an American?

Given the rather heavy intellectual sledding we have been going through, I want to shift gears for a moment and do something fun. I want to try to define what it means to be an American. Now, given the diversity of the population, experiences, and viewpoints, this obviously isn't going to be very precise. No two Americans agree on all issues, so this cannot be an analysis of politics. Here is my short list of what makes us Americans:

1. We put liberty above tribe.
2. We enjoy diversity of viewpoint;
3. We like our privacy, and we don't like busybodies.
4. We have a streak of the do-gooder in us (I call it Dudley Do-Rightism).
5. We are forgiving, and we believe in second chances.
6. We believe in the rule of law.
7. We are pragmatic.

8. We look up to money, fame, and power, but we believe in the virtue of the everyman.
9. We believe in the market system, to varying degrees.
10. We like a healthy optimism.
11. We may exhibit bigotry sometimes, but we don't think highly of it, at least not publicly.

When I think of great Americans, I think of John Adams, James Madison, Alexander Hamilton, Thomas Jefferson, George Washington, Abraham Lincoln, Calvin Coolidge, Ronald Reagan, Louis Brandeis, William Rehnquist, Martin Luther King, Thomas Edison, Edward Hopper, George Gershwin, Walt Disney, Gene Roddenberry, and Stephen Spielberg, among others. Of course, there are many people lost to history who were probably terrific, hardworking patriots. America is a place where dreams can come true for some people if they have luck and the right stuff in their heads. I still believe that America is the greatest country in history. But we've got some work to do. As Zbigniew Brzezinski has pointed out in his book *Strategic Vision: America and the Crisis of Global Power* (2012), if we want to lead the world, we must do so by example; and to do that, we have to put our own house in order. The hardest question that we are facing is whether our political system is able to do that because some pain will be involved in our course correction. Although President Obama claimed that "good policy is good politics," he is wrong. Sometimes good policy is horrible politics. Won't fixing the entitlement programs make someone angry? Remember when the angry townspeople come after the Frankenstein monster with torches and pitchforks and you will have an idea about what is likely to happen.

Intelligence and Education

There are some dumb people, and there are some geniuses, but most people fall in a range in which they are smart enough to understand most of what they need to in order to function in the workplace. A much bigger problem than a lack of intelligence is a lack of knowledge. It is hard to make good decisions unless you possess the right information. It is hard to be competent if you don't read.

I am a big believer in the KISS rule: keep it simple, stupid. I think that higher-level thinking is simple, such as Bill Gates's vision of "a computer on every desktop in the world" and the four-note motif that dominates the first movement of the Beethoven Fifth Symphony. Simple, but not simpleminded.

It is not true that people who are rich are smarter than those who are not, at least not in every case. University professors are often smart, but not very rich. Sometimes people who are not smart get rich through hard work and a lot of luck. Sometimes smart people like to stay below the radar so that their jobs are safer because they are risk averse. As a result, station in life or rank isn't the whole story. Albert Einstein was a patent clerk, but he was far smarter than most CEOs. Also, rank can change over time, and people retire eventually; so in the end, you will be judged on your brain and your character. Don't fall for the trappings of success. Fame is fleeting.

Having a good job in which you deal with complex issues can help your brain develop. This may explain part of the lagging intellectual or artistic achievements of women or minorities prior to the twentieth century (pure speculation on my part). I think that there are many different types of intelligence. Gustav Mahler is my favorite composer, but as a young boy, he was near the bottom of his class. Education raises many difficult questions. Does the use of the scientific method and data collection make sense in the context of something as touchy-feely as teaching? Does pay for performance make sense if the teacher has limited impact and measurement is difficult? Does a one-sized fits all approach make any sense in education? Is a poor kid stupid because he is poor or because poor people tend to be stupid in the first place? Or is poverty partly about the inability to access good information? Or is it simply a function of whether your parents and siblings cared enough about you to interact with you and thereby stimulate your brain? Are more rules or more freedom the way forward?

Education is a process—we know that—but at what point does it start to have diminishing returns?

Pianist Josef Lhévinne made a key point:

> The teacher of beginners is a person of great importance in all education, particularly in music. In Russia the teacher of the beginners is often a man or woman of real distinction. The work is not looked upon as an ignoble one, worthy of only the failures or the inferior teachers. These teachers are well paid. (*Basic Principles in Pianoforte Playing* 1972, 2)

Of course, this applies beyond music to all studies. I'm not sure that Americans are sufficiently divorced from their "lifestyles of the rich and famous" ethos to get their priorities straight. To attract people to the teaching profession, we have to avoid thinking in terms like "those who can do, those who can't teach." I thought that as kid, and it is nonsense. It is better to say that sometimes there are people who can do but can't teach it for diddly. I can play the piano, but I have absolutely no idea how to teach someone else to do it.

It is a cliché that you need to have sports in school to teach teamwork, punctuality, and hard work. Baseball—as Al Capone (played by Robert De Niro) in the movie *The Untouchables* points out—teaches both individual achievement, when you are at bat, and teamwork, when you are fielding. Basketball teaches that not everyone can make the slam dunk and that the guy who does an assist by passing the ball to his teammate, who gets the glory, is just as important. But let us not forget golf, which for obvious reasons isn't prevalent in public schools. Golf teaches you to play your own game and ignore what your competitors are doing because it can throw you off.

Art and music are important to education as well. Art teaches you to have an eye for beauty, which you need when you are doing design work, architecture, engineering, and even when drafting legislation. Art is also fun and may promote creativity. Music helps with concentration, visualization, memory, and verbal fluency. I can't prove that, but I think it. The ancient Greeks thought music was part of a basic education, and maybe we shouldn't discount that kind of ancient wisdom without evidence. Also, we should foster appreciation for art and music because these are the things that help justify human existence. You are not going to justify humanity based on our ability to put gas in everyone's car or make excellent helicopter gunships, are you? Finally, art and music are artifacts of history that reflect the cultures and the time that created them. If you want to see into the past, it is not just a matter of knowing the date of the Battle of Trafalgar. You want to know how these people thought. They were humans like us, of course, but their world views may have been very different indeed.

War

I wrote about war policy in my book *Basic Stuff That Everyone Should Know*. I think I did an acceptable job of summarizing the key points, although I did unwittingly adopt the military-industrial and foreign policy establishment's philosophy that we need a big military to an extent I probably shouldn't have. I really don't think war is as easy to wage today as it was in the past. The disparity in military power has equalized somewhat between various nations as more have modernized and technology has spread. There are video cameras in every cell phone and rapid posting of videos to social media, and this makes prolonged violence or major destruction difficult politically. There is now an international law system of our own creation that didn't exist in the old days. We now have a bankrupt treasury. We have far less manufacturing capacity than we did before. We have a volunteer army instead of a draft army. We use rigid rules of engagement that might hamper victory. We fight some nongovernmental entities (i.e., terrorists) instead of nation states that are easier to bomb. We exhibit less racism and cultural elitism than before (at least superficially). All of these things make it harder for us to achieve our ends through war.

We should ponder the extent to which morality and war go together. Carl von Clausewitz emphasized that, at bottom, war is killing. In other words, it ain't beanbag. I think that when you kill your enemies, you must do so with impunity. But we do need to maintain the morale of our troops and the support of the public, and if people feel that their cause is moral, it will help. I think we are still not sure about what we should use war for. The just war doctrine goes back to Aquinas. Cap Weinberger created criteria for going to war. But those are dated. Here is my own checklist, which I suggest should be run before going to war:

1. What is the goal of the war?
2. What is the moral justification of the war? Do we fight to help ourselves or others?
3. What is the national security interest that is served?
4. Is the war absolutely necessary or merely advisable?
5. Is there a military solution, or are political, diplomatic, or economic solutions required?
6. How do we define what victory looks like?
7. Can victory be achieved as a practical matter?
8. At what cost can victory be achieved?

9. How long will it take to achieve victory?
10. Do we have the financial ability to fight the war?
11. Do we have the will and the public and political commitment to see the war to victory?
12. Have less destructive and workable alternatives been tried?

The public will support war more fully if they believe that the decision was made according to a logical process. The thing that disturbs me most about war is when politicians who have run away from military service in the past act tough and warlike. Chicken hawks, they are called. It is easy to act tough when you are not the one who has to fight. I never liked men with something to prove (or women, for that matter). Of course, it is fun to talk tough; and I do it from time to time, but I'm not sure it comes from a place of strength. Some of our great war hawks were probably the kind of kids who had their lunch money stolen.

One of my relatives by marriage was a real war hero, but you would have never known it because he was modest and seemed like the softest, quietest guy. He didn't talk about his war experience the way some do today. I take my cues from that type of person. I also think there is something to the notion that if we still had the draft, it would be harder to go to war because the burdens would fall more broadly across the voting public. War is bad all around, and as historian Paul Johnson has said, it results in moral degradation on both sides (see his book *Modern Times*). That said, we cannot take war off the table as an option because weakness invites aggression. To maintain a credible threat, we need to have the will to use our military. If we do not, then all of our military spending adds up to nothing. Please note that a threat is sometimes better than action, if the action is a failure and destroys your credibility. Also, there can be a bad slippery slope in war, as we saw in Vietnam, where you keep doubling down on a failed policy just to maintain your credibility. In the end, that may have the opposite effect.

Personally, I'm not keen on having women serve in forward combat infantry units if the commanders think it doesn't work as a practical matter. That said, it depends on the kind of team you're building. If you have a woman who has a little less strength but is an expert marksman, then maybe you should put her on the team. Also, I see no reason to keep women from flying aircraft in combat; and of course, they have been doing that for quite a while.

In his book on Vietnam, *Dispatches*, Michael Herr quoted a veteran who said that "greasing people was the greatest thrill of my life." *The New York Times* reported on a helicopter gunship pilot in Iraq who said that he got an erection when he was firing his weapons on people on the ground. People like to play God, let's admit that. We just need to be aware of this aspect of human nature. It can be very useful when killing bad guys, but it can be dysfunctional when making the policy decision to go to war. Some guys, like Nazis, are worth killing; and if we do that, we shouldn't have to feel endlessly guilty about it. The fact is that it is hard to be good at something unless you enjoy doing it, at least a little bit. Understand, I fully support the dedicated people who serve voluntarily in our armed forces and put their own personal interests beneath a higher purpose. I'm not saying they are all depraved maniacs who get into the business because they enjoy hurting people. I have a high regard for them. I'm just reporting on an aspect of human nature that we all know exists—in latent form, to some extent—in many people, if not in all people.

Finally, in an era where preemptive war has been used for so-called defensive purposes, we should recall World War II. Did we get involved to save Europe, to protect democracy and freedom, to save the Jews from extinction? Nope, the Japanese bombed Pearl Harbor, and shortly thereafter, Hitler declared war on the United States. We didn't exactly have a choice. By the end of World War II, we had a little over twelve million troops under uniform. That was the kind of commitment needed to win. One thing we have learned about to a dead certainty: war is nothing to play at.

Government, Business, and Economics

In almost every election, some businessman claims that he wants to run government like a business. In my books *Reinventing Government: A Practitioner's Guide* and *Basic Stuff That Everyone Should Know*, I debunk this idea. I don't want to restate that entire exposition, but everyone should understand that there is a big difference between a government monopoly, which is tax funded and serves everyone regardless of the ability to pay, and a business, which only serves people who choose to pay and have the option to buy from other businesses. This fundamental difference in purpose means that management policies that might work in one situation won't work in another.

If I had to bring it down to a single point, I would say that the biggest difference between a business owner and a government manager is that a businessman will cut off activity as soon as he sees that it is not going be productive whereas a government manager may not—because for the business owner, activity means time and money out of his own pocket.

Also, in comparing government and business solutions, we must recognize that because all actions by government must be enabled by law, it is necessarily more rule bound and inflexible than most businesses, although this varies somewhat by business type and size. A big bank that is heavily regulated can be almost as bureaucratic as a government agency. Now, on this point about the government as a monopoly, all great economists of the past have agreed that some things are public goods that government should provide on a monopoly basis. The policy issue is, exactly which things?

Sometimes public-private partnerships sound like a good idea, but it depends on how they are set up and who the private partner is. John Locke advocated for the separation of church and state because he worried about the corruption of one by the other flowing in both directions (see Locke, *A Letter Concerning Toleration*). The same can sometimes be true of public-private partnerships, although it sort of depends on the situation and setup. Across the world, there are different approaches—from communism where the business is owned by the government, to industrial policy where the government helps to direct the strategic objectives of the business, to public-private partnerships, to tax incentives and grants, to a relatively free market where the government only provides a level playing field. It is very complex to analyze the difference between different types of models, but at least I would be willing to say that excessive government is problematic.

The extreme case of North Korea versus South Korea strongly suggests that there are some benefits provided by the market system. Also, I want to point out that while some American liberals like to point to Europe as an example of a good society that has a top-heavy government and nice benefits, we should recognize that the United States is subsidizing their defense needs in a big way, and this helps the European models succeed. In building governance structures, a mix of centralization and decentralization is needed and perhaps cannot be avoided. The law firm that I worked in had around two hundred lawyers, but each section was its own profit center that did its own hiring and firing. Our federalist system of federal and state government in America is a good example of this mixture of centralization plus decentralization. I think it works pretty well, but sometimes excessive federal micromanagement can cause problems. There is always a balance.

In my book *Basic Stuff That Everyone Should Know*, I tried to summarize the basics of economics in a short chapter. I'm not going to repeat that. It is enough to say that, at bottom, economics boils down to the allocation of resources through the price mechanism and the interaction of supply and demand. Adam Smith's insight that we call the *invisible hand* was that individuals independently pursuing their own self-interest would end up magically increasing the economic benefits accruing to everyone. It is a policy of decentralization and freedom. More modernly we have faced the question of whether we can maintain the right level of aggregate demand in a developed economy that is driven about 70 percent by consumption despite the fact that a significant part of that consumption is discretionary at the same time that we have low workforce participation and serious income inequality.

As Joseph Stigliz has pointed out, income inequality can harm aggregate demand (see Stigliz, *The Great Divide: Unequal Societies and What We Can Do About Them* 2015). Now, I think most businesspeople know that they want customers with money to spend, and having a lot of poor people running around isn't in their interests. I also think that it is archaic to think that rich people make money by stealing it from poor people. There is some "trickle up" as people spend money, and it flows to business owners. But our economy is not a zero-sum game because the overall pie can grow, and some money goes to workers in the form of salaries. I am not poorer because Bill Gates is richer.

The key economics point is that we want to have a system that incentivizes productivity at the same time that it distributes the spoils in a way that doesn't work against those incentives. This is a complex question. Taxing away too much money from the rich could harm business formation, innovation, hiring, and investment—particularly if those rich happen to be part of the creative class of innovators (not all are). But if the middle class, working class, and poor can't get ahead, then what incentive do they have to work hard for? Similarly, if discrimination bars minorities and women from access to good jobs, then what incentive do they have to work hard? We need to think carefully through the balance between growing the pie and carving up the pie. In addition, we need to improve the inputs to the economy, such as education. Whether that is possible is not clear, but our task is very clear: K-12 is not up to snuff and needs some work. Higher education is the envy of the world, but it is getting to be cost prohibitive.

A few of the quotes in the preface to this book pertain to the question of the role of government and the economy and the underlying culture. The key is to realize that the law plays some role in an economy. One reason is because businesses and individuals need the law to protect their interests. But a larger reason is that businesses need to plan in an uncertain world, and a consistent rule of law helps them to do that. That is why law enforcement is not just about cops and robbers but also about jobs and money.

Since I have been a business lawyer and regulator, one of my pet peeves is free marketeers who don't understand that the market doesn't know everything because the market is made up of people and information doesn't flow that easily. If the market knows about something, it can react quickly, but there is a lot that it doesn't know about. In my book *Reinventing Government: A Practitioner's Guide*, I talk about the economics of regulation. The main takeaway is that business regulation isn't necessarily bad, although excessive micromanagement by rules is generally not a good idea. We should remember the relatively recent history of deregulation of the savings and loans and the repeal of the Glass-Steagall Act, both of which resulted in disaster. It isn't good to apply simplistic theories about economics to an economic reality that is far more complex than that. In addition, the fact that an economics PhD like Senator Phil Gramm doesn't understand that bank finance, the lifeblood of our economy, might present a different case for regulation than a hardware store or a flower shop shows that an academic degree is no guarantee of common sense. In a similar vein, many of us believe in the power of competition, but pure competition doesn't exist in some areas of the economy, particularly in situations where you are not paying your own way or your "purchase" isn't voluntary or discretionary. In other words, one has to look at the facts of the case at hand.

We should also recognize that complex business regulation can favor larger businesses over smaller businesses and established businesses over start-ups. In addition, if regulation makes it harder to operate a business, doesn't that hurt the less educated, and doesn't that have a bad effect on the overall economy? But people should stop saying that all regulation is antibusiness. In finance, regulation helps increase consumer confidence in the finance system so that money will continue to flow in. That is proindustry. The basic debate about regulation is simple: if people are stupid, do we need more rules, or is the government too stupid to create and administer rules? In thinking about that, remember that you need some basic government and law to create a good market, such as property rights and contract rights enforcement, security, physical infrastructure, financial infrastructure, and investment in research and development.

After the 2008 financial crisis, a lawyer asked me what I thought about the unprecedented government intervention that followed, and I said that I thought the market was self-correcting. He called me a Herbert Hoover. I should have said that the market is self-correcting over the long term and that self-correction doesn't mean that you have aggregate demand at a particular level. Well, live and learn. At that time, I was asked by an engineer what I thought would fix things. I said, "This is about faith and confidence." I think that is generally right, but perhaps today I would add a few more elements. Also, another pet peeve I have is that people do not consider whether there is really a big difference between the Democratic call for more government spending funded by debt and the Republican call for lower taxes funded by debt? Aren't both Keynesian policies? I would say that short-term stimulus might make sense, but permanent stimulus is a road to fiscal ruin.

Jeffrey Sachs has recounted the fact that some economists believe that there is a role for government in the economy. He notes,

> Samuelson's great synthesis called on market forces to allocate most goods in the economy, while

> calling on governments to perform three essential tasks: redistributing income to protect the poor and the unlucky; providing public goods such as infrastructure and scientific research; and stabilizing the macroeconomy. (*The Price of Civilization: Reawakening American Virtue and Prosperity* 2011, 29)

We should also consider the contrarian views of Nassim Nicholas Taleb:

> So I disagree with the followers of Marx and those of Adam Smith; the reason free markets work is because they allow people to be lucky, thanks to aggressive trial and error, not by giving rewards or "incentives" for skill. The strategy is, then, to tinker as much as possible and try to collect as many Black Swan opportunities as you can. (*Black Swan* 2010, xxv)

I would like to suggest a few generalizations about economics for the reader:

1. Economics is not a science, and it can be too theoretical.
2. Economists who stick closer to the facts are better than those who are too theoretical.
3. The success of a particular economic policy depends on the context (the situation at hand).
4. Economic policy won't work unless people believe it will work and it affects their behavior.

5. Economics involves so many variables that policy can be hard to analyze.
6. Change is the constant, and what succeeded yesterday may not succeed tomorrow.
7. Economists usually make statements under the assumption "all other things being equal" and they never are.
8. Economics predictions about a specific policy can be wrong because our thinking can be too simplistic as compared to the reality of the world.
9. There are different kinds of capitalism. The sole proprietor world of Adam Smith is not the same as today's world of big corporations.

In addition, I want to show the reader the checklist for drafting legislation that I came up with in the wake of the Affordable Care Act and the Dodd-Frank Act, both of which are way too long and way too complicated to be practical. Law affects the economy, so economists should take an interest in how we make laws. Here is my legislative drafting checklist:

1. Define the problem to be solved.
2. Define the means to be used to solve the problem.
3. Check to see that each of the means solves the problem.
4. Check to see if the solution is total or partial.

5. Check to see if the solution is really needed in light of existing federal and state law.
6. Remember that it is easier to tell people not to do something than to require affirmative action.
7. Consider the benefits of simplicity versus complexity in your solution.
8. Avoid micromanagement.
9. Check to see if the requirements of the law are realistic—can they be done? Check theory versus practice.
10. Check to see if the requirements must change rapidly as the world changes.
11. Consider unintended consequences.
12. Consider trade-offs.
13. Consider the benefits of doing nothing instead of putting in the bill.
14. Omit unnecessary words (make the target as small as possible for your enemies).
15. Consider the political constituency for the bill.
16. Remember Calvin Coolidge's statement that "sometimes people want things they ought not to want."
17. Locate the function in the right department or agency.

Policy decisions are no different from any other decision. There are trade-offs and unintended consequences. The question is, Do you want these set of problems or those set of problems? There is no such thing as a world with no problems. If you find yourself complaining about a given policy, ask yourself what alternative you would propose. But one thing we can do to improve policy is simple: stop abusing the word processor. In the days of the Founding Fathers, when they used feather-pen-and-ink and block printing, they would never have considered a one-thousand-page bill like Obamacare. Laziness increases efficiency.

I spoke to a CEO of a start-up biotech firm, and he said the same thing that the CEO of Dow Chemical said. They would prefer that any regulation coming down from the government would tell them what the goals were but leave the method to them. I told him that rules didn't necessarily work that way because we have a need to do enforcement. But it is not impossible to do what the CEO said some of the time. For example, under the Affordable Care Act, an incentive for hospitals receiving federal reimbursements was created based on improvements in readmission rates, but they left the question of how to the hospitals. As another example, one bad thing about the Affordable Care Act or, more properly, the way they implemented it is that they put too much specificity into the requirements for the exchanges; and this increased the costs and complexities, particularly as it related to IT. The question then is really how much specificity to put into a statute? Or, as I suggest in the checklist, maybe we should avoid affirmative mandates that force people to do and implement things.

In the Preface, I have cited a few pithy statements on institutions, culture, and society. Let me say this: our system is somewhat malleable, but not completely malleable. We do things for a reason, at least most of the time. Also, we cannot just get up one morning and entirely change our culture and identities. We cannot change human nature. Special interests have power. So if you are going to try to change the system, you need to understand the system first so that you do no harm. Calvin Coolidge said that the business of the American people is business, and that is more or less true. If legislation passes, it is often because it helps business at the same time it helps the disadvantaged. This coalition can be powerful, which is partly why Ronald Reagan was right when he said that "the closest thing to eternal life that we know is a government program." Once you put legislation in place, it can be very hard to reverse.

You may want to Google the lyrics for Stephen Sondheim and Leonard Bernstein's song "Gee, Officer Krupke" from *West Side Story*. Sondheim is a genius, and he captures the debate we are still having between the Right and the Left about whether people are the product of nature or nurture and how you solve social problems and whether you can hold people responsible for their own behavior. I'm not sure that we are ever going to know how much is nature and how much is nurture, so in the end, the question is what government policy produces the best results as a practical matter.

One of the most important concepts I learned in college was by reading Bernard Williams's work on moral luck. Essentially, he is saying that some people are just luckier than others and their success is not exclusively about their own achievement. I believe strongly in luck, although I justify it by saying that God decides these things for his own reasons that we cannot understand because we do not know the overall plan. The concept of moral luck is important for policy because too many rich people take credit for building the whole railroad by themselves. My father was a businessman; and he attributed most of his success to being in the United States of America and, as an early Asian property developer, by being in Hawaii. I think his attitude is the correct one. A little humility and gratitude go a long way.

Another key philosophical point is the question of whether the government should be used to do good Christian works or not. I don't think the Bible says that, but there could be a reasonable debate about it. Using other people's money to be charitable might not be as godly as some might think. Some people think redistribution of income is theft. Of course, in a way, all government spending involves redistribution, so the argument proves too much and is politically untenable for almost anyone, but pundit

Jonathan Hoenig, that is—a gutsy and principled guy but with a view from the cheap seats.

As to money, it makes the world go round as the song from *Cabaret* says. If we didn't use money, we'd be a lot poorer, let me tell you. To me, money is morally neutral. Andrew Carnegie made huge money and became a great philanthropist. On the other hand, gangsters who kill for drug money or who make money off prostitutes who don't get a fair share are evil. We should examine the Christian critique carefully, though. They do not say that money is evil. They say that money is the root of all evil, which is to say that it has that potential. Greed is one of the seven deadly sins, but not all people who have money are greedy. Greed implies an excessive attachment to money. I am frugal and tightfisted, but some people consider me generous in my willingness to give gifts and make charitable contributions. I don't think that I have an unhealthy relationship toward money. It is a tool, and it can solve some problems, but that is all. Indeed, if you are allowing money to distort your behavior excessively, that might not be a good thing. As Hal Holbrook says to Charlie Sheen in the movie *Wall Street*, "That's the problem with money, Bud. It makes you do things that you don't want to do."

Some people want to improve the government by cutting salaries or downsizing. But ask yourself this, if we fired half of the state and local employees in your area, would that be good for local business? If we cut government, we do not know if the private sector economy would expand to fill the entire gap that is left behind. What if the money saved from cutting government just goes into people's bank accounts? Not all will, of course, but you get the point.

One man's costs are another man's revenues. One man's rights are another man's liabilities. In other words, when you do public policy, often there are winners and there are losers. The win-win scenario all the way around isn't that common.

Should government help business? Remember that there is a difference between helping a single business and helping all businesses across the board. The latter is good policy. If you do the former, you might be accused of corruption. Now, the kind of corruption we have in the United States is not even on the same scale as in other countries. But economists have figured out that the rule of law and the reduction of corruption are important to the health of an economy. So it is not just a matter of skirting the rules a bit here or there. It is a matter of jobs and money, at least in the ultimate analysis. I have said that before, but it such an important point that I don't mind saying it again.

When doing public policy, remember that just because someone is an underdog doesn't mean that he is better than the people currently in power. Some of these underdogs are dangerous. Look at how Robespierre acted once he took power. He turned into "Mr. Guillotine."

One of the basic problems that we have is that we are atomized individuals who can't read one another's minds and who are physically cut off from one another. As a result, we sometimes do not have an effective feedback loop for our public policies. Fortunately, computer technology allows us to create feedback solutions. But we would have to train ourselves to use them.

How about another pet peeve? Mitt Romney said famously that "corporations are people too, my friend." That is a lawyer answer, but it is a legal fiction. Corporations are not people. If they were, you could marry one and have children with it. I understand why our Supreme Court thinks that corporations should have some protected First Amendment rights around speech, campaign contributions, and religion; but I don't think they absolutely had to go down that path because we can all see how real human beings and corporations are not exactly the same thing. I hope that I go to heaven, and I sure hope I don't see Exxon Mobil standing in front of me in line to see St. Peter. The fact is, they have helped a lot more people than I have. How's that for a little corporatist humor?

Government can be different from business in the lack of immediacy of feedback. In business, if you don't please your customers, you probably will go out of business. Government is a bit more impervious. Sometimes government people find it too easy to ignore the world swirling around them. If businesspeople do that, they die quickly. Also, government is, in a way, too idealistic. One must always remember then that the public doesn't care about intentions; they care about results. They don't care about ideas; they care about execution. For example, I may put up a big Christmas tree and cover it with beautiful lights and ornaments, but when I go to extend the electric cord to meet the electric socket and it doesn't reach, then my execution has failed. You can have big, beautiful ideas and visions, but making it happen means thinking through the details. Make sure the damn thing works.

By now it is almost a cliché that most of our big public policy problems are related to one another and cannot be analyzed unless we look at them all together. Very true, but it is not clear that you should solve all of them at the same time or that each problem is of equal importance. For example, if we could fix education, that would have a huge ripple effect on other problems. In addition, not all these problems can be solved in the same way. Some may be better solved by government, others by business, others by nonprofits, others by community volunteers, or some by a combination of the aforementioned. The most important reason why we must teach people that the big problems are connected is that sometimes people do not realize that they are affected by what happens to some other people who live far away. People do not always know that they are in the same boat. Not caring about your fellow man can hurt you. Integrating policy across the board can be tricky.

Something might make sense as a stand-alone policy, but not in the context of other policies. For example, can you hold people to personal responsibility for their success in life if you have a bad public education system? Can you advocate for an estate tax of zero as part of a larger program to cut back on government welfare services at the same time that you want rich people to give part of their estate to charitable purposes?

Some studies show that conservatives are more fearful of danger than liberals. Could be. When it comes to the economy, liberals seem convinced that no matter what kinds of debt or regulation they impose, it won't harm the economy. Conservatives seem to be very paranoid about an economic engine they see as rather fragile. There are a lot of things that can go wrong, but I will talk about a few:

1. Small losses in GDP growth like 1 percent a year may seem small, but over a decade or more, they can add up to a substantially lower standard of living.
2. Oil is important to the economy not just because it powers our cars but because we need cars and trucks to move product to retail outlets. Thus, if a terrorist could remove a substantial part of the Middle Eastern oil-production capacity from the market, the effect on prices here in America might be devastating.

3. Cyber attacks are not just bad for the data that is compromised but because of the damage to consumer confidence and the barrier to entry it erects for those who wish to start a small business.
4. The electrical grid may be too vulnerable. Of course, we can't live for long without power. We simply are not configured to "rough it" anymore.
5. Big disasters, whether caused by Mother Nature or evil terrorists, can have a profound effect on the American economy.
6. The federal debt is too big and growing fast. Because debt is abstract, people can sometimes have a hard time understanding how it affects us. Big federal debt makes future generations subsidize older generations. Big federal debt destroys the confidence of consumers to buy and businesses to hire and invest. Big federal debt will crowd out other worthy programs for the poor and downtrodden, and it could crowd out important defense spending. Big federal debt that produces high interest rates can wreak havoc with the economy and the world of investments.

Law Pointers

In my book *Basic Stuff That Everyone Should Know*, I talk a bit about law basics. I won't repeat that exposition. The main question for this new book is, How should business owners or managers handle lawyers? I am lucky in the sense that because I am both a business guy and a lawyer, the synergy between the two happens automatically. I say lucky, but my mother planned for me to become a business guy with a law degree because she ran a small business, and she knew that dealing with lawyers was a big part of it. In the movie *Godfather II*, Michael Corleone (played by Al Pacino) says, "My father taught me, keep your friends close but your enemies closer." This applies to lawyers. A lawyer deprived of information from his client cannot function as a lawyer because the law is not about rules as much as it is about facts considered in the context of rules.

In my capacity as a business lawyer, I think of myself as performing a risk-management function. I cannot eliminate risk, but I will try to reduce it through foresight.

This marks the difference between corporate law work and litigation. The corporate lawyer looks forward to a future of possible multiple fact patterns. The litigator looks backward to something that happened in the past, and the facts are fixed, even if there may be a dispute over what they are. Please don't blame your lawyer for everything. The person best suited to avoiding problems is a manager making business or policy decisions, not a lawyer. If you want your lawyer to succeed in court, then don't hand him or her a bad fact pattern. It's your fact pattern. Take responsibility for it. The lawyer takes the facts as he or she finds them, at least in litigation as I have said.

Also, remember that when you go to court, you can expect procedural justice, but it is harder to get substantive justice. Outcomes can be unpredictable. The main thing is not to sue in anger. Think of it as a business decision. And remember that most cases settle before trial anyway, so the sooner you settle, the better for you, although not for your lawyer. If you are suing someone, try to go on a contingency fee and not hourly fees so that you get better alignment of the lawyer with your interests.

Watch out for lawyers who trade on their surface appearance. In the end, what matters is what is inside the cranium. Of course, trial law is a bit different from most types of law, which are more like desk jobs. There is a theatrical quality to trial work, and you do have to dress the part and cut your hair and things like that. I know one trial lawyer who will wear a beard for some cases and not for others. That's how superficial it can be in court because the decision-makers, be they judges or juries, may judge people in part by surface appearances (although I'm not sure if that beard thing is just superstition on the part of that particular lawyer).

If you are going to sue someone, ask yourself if you will make a sympathetic plaintiff because the emotions of the judge or jury will come into play. As a thirteen-year-old testifying in court, I got pounded by a judge who resented the fact that our lawyer had made a big deal of the fact that I went to a private school. Also, remember that litigation is slow and unpleasant and can take a toll on your family; so unless fairly big money is involved, it might be better to stay out of court.

If you get sued for negligence, it might be based more on your procedures than the substantive decision you made. So try to use good procedures and document those procedures. That said, one mistake that some nonlawyers make is that they overcompensate for potential liability because they are not able to weigh the danger of being sued. Others do the opposite. Some people think that nothing bad can happen to them because they are nice people. Wrong. Sometimes prosecutors and lawyers can be rather ruthless. Sometimes they seem to be part reptile.

Now, a word on the philosophy of law. In government, I was asked by a caller why he had to pay a particular fee.

I said, "Because that's the law." He said, "That sounds very superficial, Mr. Lim." He was a doctor, you see, and rather moralistic. But his question is an interesting one that deserves a little discussion.

Some thinkers grounded this question in authority or sovereignty. This idea originated at a time of monarchies. Some thinkers believe that law is a function of social norms, which are themselves a function of the economic, political, and historical situation. Some thinkers believe that law is tied to natural law or morality or God's law. This idea makes more sense with respect to some laws than others. In addition, natural law might justify the basic idea for a statute, but much of the details might be harder to tie to the underlying natural law. Man-made law is usually called positive law. I have heard a few people call man-made law *common law*. Not true. Common law is judge-made law, and it is to be contrasted with civil law systems. My own view is that in the United States government, power is rooted in the consent of the governed and that if a law has met the procedural requirements for passing a law, including the Constitution, then it is valid.

As to using a lawyer for contract negotiations, this won't happen unless you are doing a big deal. Otherwise, it will be a form document. If you negotiate, remember that leverage is important, which often means that he who has the gold makes the rules and that he who has more time can exert pressure on he who is in more of a hurry. Also, if you want a good deal, you need to be able to walk away, and you should have an understanding of what your counterparty's financial end is. In order to understand your counterparty's interests, listening is key.

Businesspeople sometimes say that if you have five lawyers in a room, you will get five different opinions. That is true sometimes, but it is not always true, and perhaps not even often true. Some legal issues are in the gray area while some are black-and-white. Not everything is the same thing, as I keep trying to explain to people. It is good for lawyers to try to stretch a bit to find a way for their client to do what they want to do; but at some point, if you stretch too far, the law will break. It is a major disservice for a lawyer to tell you that you can do something when you can't. That said, there is often some gray area. Consider, for example, the difference between a legal opinion that says that a court *would* hold that x, versus that a court *should* hold that x, versus that a court *could* hold that x. In other words, there are varying degrees of legal certainty.

Another common misconception about lawyers is that they are all created equal and are all smart. A governor whom I will not name was speaking before a group of lawyers, and he started off by saying, "You're lawyers, right? That means that some of you are of above average intelligence." I laughed at that joke, but not everyone did. Lawyers come in all shapes and sizes, and they all have different backgrounds. The law today rewards extreme specialization in part because the law is so vast that no one lawyer can know it all. So when you are looking for a lawyer, do your homework. And for Pete's sake, don't fall for the marketing ploy that a lawyer who charges high fees must be good. Remember also that your lawyer will drive your law stuff. Under the usual ethics rules, clients determine objectives, but the lawyers determine the means. The exception is where the lawyer is spending your money or when the lawyer is getting you in big trouble. For those things, they need consent.

You may remember the Sidney Lumet movie *The Verdict*, where Paul Newman—playing a broken-down, has-been lawyer—rejects a settlement offer without consulting his client. That would never happen in real life because it is a gross violation of any code of professional responsibility. Screenwriter David Mamet took that bit of artistic license because without it, there would be no movie. You may have forgotten, but the American Bar Association had bad things to say about the portrayal of lawyers in that movie.

Judicial activism versus restraint or strict constructionism is in the eye of the beholder. But you cannot call a judge a judicial activist just because you don't agree with a given decision. If you believe in the rule of law, you must accept the good with the bad so long as the process was valid. I think of a conservative judge as one who is somewhat deferential to a legislature (although I admit there can be a "spirit of law versus letter of law" question that throws off the analysis). Anyway, I don't know why some people want judges to be partisan. It would be better if they just did straight analysis.

Now, I want to tell a few stories about lawyers, at the risk of sounding petty. We actually have a rule of professional responsibility that we are not supposed to put the profession in a bad light. But I am not telling these stories to make fun of lawyers but to show the kinds of human frailty that can masquerade as professionalism.

When I was in my second year at UCLA law school, I had a job interview with the federal Department of Justice. I talked to an appellate lawyer who looked a bit like Justice Stephen Breyer, so I figured he was smart. He asked me what I had majored in at Columbia. I said, "English." He said, "English language?" I said, "English literature." Yeah, nice question. Later I was making a point, and I used the word *distinct*. He said, "Discrete." Well, you can look it up in the dictionary. These two words are synonyms.

Another fun guy was a deputy attorney general in Hawaii whom I worked with a lot. He always insisted on correcting my punctuation. He insisted that there should always be a comma before a conjunction, as in "animals, birds, and fish." In fact, there is a split of authority on this point. Strunk & White call for the comma before the conjunction; Warriner's does not. When there is a split of authority on grammar like this, it might be okay to advise the way this lawyer did, but not to insist. Also, it clearly makes no difference in terms of legal consequences, so why is a lawyer giving this kind of advice?

For my own part, I don't think many readers are so stupid that they can't figure out that there is a space between the words. The conjunction tells them that, even if there is no comma precedent. Finally, language is part of culture, and it changes the way any culture changes. So to look for fixed and absolute rules is a fool's errand. For example, there is a long-standing dispute in the law over whether *shall* is the same as *will*. I think so, but not everyone agrees with me. I think the issue has cultural aspects because *shall* sounds more like the Ten Commandments and therefore sounds more like a command, even if it isn't different in substance. Again, I'm not making fun of lawyers per se. I'm making fun of people who are twerps and who want to be "the man" because it makes them feel good. Yeah, "get out that car and put your hands on the hood so I can feel you up." You know the type.

One of the problems with a world full of lawyers is that the liability makes it harder for us to admit error and take responsibility. Just be aware as a businessperson that, once in a blue moon, you may have to push your lawyers' concerns about liability aside in order to take responsibility for your actions and maintain your credibility with the public. Sometimes it is not enough leadership to simply say, "No comment."

Partisanship

We're all utterly sick and tired of the partisan bickering in America. At the core of the problem is a delusional fallacy in the minds of many politicians. Here's the thinking. If the other party is dangerous to America's future, then our party must take power or stay in power; and to do that, I must win my particular election. Therefore, anything I can do to achieve that is A-OK. This equating of individual self-interest with the national interest is at the root of our problems. The invisible hand works in economics, but not in politics. The other difficulty we have is that, for a long time, politicians have been buying votes; and as a result, fixing our fiscal crisis is going to be nearly impossible politics. Politicians also delude themselves that they are doing things for the public even though the public has no idea what they are doing. In other words, politicians sometimes avoid personal responsibility and blame the public for the things they are doing. "I did it for you, so don't blame me."

Nice. Self-serving to the extreme. Nail yourself to the cross, why don't you?

These problems are fixable if we can elect politicians who believe in family, God, and country. And of course, it helps to have some kind of a spine.

We are complicit in these problems. Our government is a reflection of ourselves. If politicians take our money to turn around and buy our votes, it is because we allow it to happen. If politicians give us speeches that dress up goals in the clothing of solutions and we eat it up like it was prime rib, then we bear some responsibility. If we can't handle the truth and we can't stand any pain because we are weak, pampered, selfish, and unpatriotic—then whose fault is that? If we don't bother to read and keep up with current events, then how can we expect our elected officials to be responsive? If we continue to believe that politicians can give us more stuff for less money, then how can we expect a responsible fiscal policy? In other words, if the lambs being taken to the slaughter are silent, then can they not expect the worst?

Also, we need to confront the question, Does it make sense to stand on principle without any regard for the practical consequences of that principle or without providing any solution for those consequences? I'm not going to answer that. It is just something that needs to be considered.

Technology and Politics

We all know that technology has always been transformative of our lives and societies. I have no doubt there is a huge pile of academic writing on that already. But it is worth focusing in on how technology has changed our politics.

In the movie *Back to the Future*, Dr. Emmett Brown (played by Christopher Lloyd) says, "Now I know why your president has to be a movie actor. He needs to look good on television." Hilarious line but, in a way, not funny. Could Abraham Lincoln be elected today with his not-exactly-a-movie-star looks and his high-pitched voice? The implications of that are scary. Also, does this aspect deter people of good character from political service at the same time that it attracts people of poor character? Another big change is that today we can do polling, and polling results influence policy. Back in the early days of the republic, it wasn't very easy to talk to one's constituents. No cell phones, no telegraphs—basically it was letters delivered by horse, or you had to go back home and talk face-to-face. So back in the old days, it was a true republic in that we had representative democracy.

Polling starts to look more like direct democracy. Given the speed associated with modern polling and the twenty-four-hour news cycle, technology has increased the likelihood that a politician will go where the wind blows. Modern communications have also made it easier to get a message to the entire nation, including remote areas; but this has increased emphasis on expensive media like television—which, in turn, raises the influence the moneyed interests can have on politicians who need big campaign contributions. That said, the Internet and social media and iPhones with video cameras create the possibility of greater accountability for politicians. The new media also may actually facilitate political discourse, more attractively called the free exchange of ideas. The other side of it is that the new technology can create even greater control over a population through monitoring, data mining, and propaganda if it were to fall into the wrong hands. Think Skynet.

Race and Culture

Bob Dylan said that the times, they are a changin'. In the past, depending on what part of the world you might be talking about, it was common for race to be contiguous with culture. But if one looks at the United States today, race and culture are not always contiguous. There is also a difference between talking about the culture of a group or area, such as the Chinese people or the United States, and talking about the culture of an individual. If I think about myself—although I was born in Hawaii, USA—I am a complex mixture of influences that can be traced back to different traditions from various parts of the world. As a result, we need to take individuals as individuals and avoid stereotypes when talking about individuals.

That said, there is a question about whether some stereotypes can be applied to groups, with the caveat that we are not talking about *all* the members of the group but *most* of them. Indeed, implied in my earlier statement that I am a hybrid of many cultural influences is the premise that some basic generalizations can be made about those cultures and the groups from which those cultures emanate. For those of you who have never studied art, music, or literature and think that there is no such thing as culture, try listening to Ravel and Bruckner and see what you think then. Remember that France and Germany share a common border and both the French and the Germans are white people from central Europe. Genetically, they cannot be radically different, but there are big cultural differences. My own view is that culture is persistent across generations, though it may fade at some point. But back to taking people as individuals. If you blame culture or race for the behavior of an individual on any given day, you are making the classic mistake of confusing correlation with causation. There are usually a lot of other factors in play.

I, for one, do not see tolerance of diversity as saying that we are all the same or that we need to be color-blind. To build a team requires people of different skills and talents, and sometimes cultural diversity can feed into that. Hawaii, where I now live and was born and raised, is ahead of the curve on diversity tolerance. That doesn't mean that there is no friction or that we don't have nasty thoughts about one another from time to time. It means that we are like an extended family, and whatever rivalries go on, we are not going to kill one another about it. Neurosurgeon Ben Carson says that it is the brain that makes you what you are. True, but what makes your brain what it is? He's sidestepping the issue a bit because his message appeals to his political base.

Racism will always be with us, or at least for the foreseeable future, but we can minimize it and work around it. Some think that the race problem is done with in America, and indeed we all know that great strides have been made. Almost everywhere the glass ceiling has been broken by at least one person of a formerly disadvantaged group. I have always marveled at the success of Oprah Winfrey. It is nothing short of a miracle that a man named Barack Hussein Obama, half black and half white, was elected president of the United States.

But racism isn't done with, and we know that because the studies of disparities in salary and wealth tell us that, even after controlling for levels of education. You, dear reader, may not be a racist; but then again, you might not have the power to hire and fire, which is where racism matters the most. We do have labor laws, but it is often difficult to prove that the reason you didn't get an interview or a callback or an offer is because of your race, gender, ethnicity, or sexual orientation. Most people who hire and fire are smart enough not to admit what they are doing, and indeed, their biases may be unknown even to them so they may not be aware of why they are making the decisions they are making.

That said, stop complaining and get on with your own life. Don't look to people for help or justice because you generally won't find any. People have their own problems to contend with. No one wants to be accused of being a racist, although a true racist is secretly proud of it. Many people are just tired of hearing about racism because some folks have just beaten the issue to death. It's not news.

Work and Meaning

I think most people derive meaning from their families and friends. Others have religious or spiritual beliefs that help them. Some, like me, have fun and interesting hobbies like playing music. But one thing that I think is a horrible development is this idea that we are supposed to derive our life's meaning and identities from our jobs. Of course, most any business and government entity in a good country like the United States helps people in some way. But that usually isn't enough because many jobs are not fun to do. I derive most of my meaning from being good at my job and doing things right and getting things done. You have to take pleasure in quality execution. It may not happen overnight, but if you work hard over a period of some years, you can develop proficiency. All businesspeople know that it is not the idea or the intention but the execution that matters to consumers. No one wants to hear, "I meant to sell you a car that didn't blow up and burn your children to death." You have to get it right. But the main point that I am making is that if you want meaning in your life, try to find it outside the office. You know, diversification?

One of the unfortunate things I heard President Obama say was that he was insulted because once someone mistook him for a parking valet. Well, what's wrong with a valet? See, that's the whole problem in a nutshell. If we don't respect people for doing an honest day's work and we look down our noses as those we outrank—even though they may be far better people than us in terms of character—then our society isn't going to work right. It is downright sinful to teach young people that some people are beneath them. Now that said, the example that President Obama provides to young black children about what is possible if you have smarts and you work hard is important to the future of America. The fact that Obama is a minority in the White House helps all minorities, regardless of how people think he is doing as a substantive matter. I don't like criticizing him in public, but this valet thing is elitism on parade. It is great that Obama inspires young people to aim high, but it is even more important for them to understand that you have to start at the bottom and work your way up. Not everyone is elevated to the top as quickly as Obama was. It is important to run a meritocracy, but we don't do that completely, and as people like Chris Hayes and William Deresciewicz have pointed out, there can be an elitist, self-justifying quality to claims of meritocracy.

People who advocate for social justice sometimes don't seem to understand that human rights is a floor. In other words, the fact that you are a human being might mean that I shouldn't kill or torture you, but it doesn't mean that I have to like and respect you. Those things have to be earned every day over a lifetime. This idea that people should be respected just because they are women or minorities is absurd and contrary to public policy because it creates a disincentive to work hard. As Mike Huckabee has said, "Equality and sameness are not the same thing." That is a deep comment. In addition, while some respect should be accorded to position, you cannot command respect if you do things that are not respectable. Anyway, if you seek high-status positions because you want respect, you are going to be disappointed. The higher up you go, the more people will try to claw you down.

To return to the original issue—work. Don't you think that a certain spiritual emptiness helps capitalism? Why buy useless trinkets and other shiny objects except to fill the horrible emotional void left by materialism? As a capitalist, I'm not sure I want people to be satisfied spiritually. I think it is bad economic policy. Similarly, while I like the Dao and other fatalistic Asian traditions, and while I like the idea that Christians should accept God's will and not ask too many questions, this kind of attitude is not going to turn you into Steve Jobs. Steve Jobs touched a lot of lives and is still doing so after he is gone. So perhaps we should be glad that he didn't go sit on a mountain and contemplate his navel the way I do. I think of myself as a labor input, and I try to have a good brand and add value to any situation. I think the idea that doing so is supposed to be about having fun is a tiny bit subversive.

Many of the people who worry about the negative psychological impact of the fact that people don't find fulfillment in their jobs seem like nice people. They may be. But if you trace this line of thinking back, it finds its origins in Marxism. Karl Marx said,

> Communism as the positive transcendence of private property, or human self-estrangement, and therefore as the real appropriation of the human essence by and for man; communism therefore as the complete return of man to himself as a social (i.e., human) being—a return become conscious, and accomplished within the entire wealth of previous development. This communism, as a fully-developed naturalism, equals humanism, and as fully-developed humanism, equals naturalism; it is the genuine resolution of the conflict between man and nature and between man and man—the true resolution of the strife between existence and essence, between objectification and self-confirmation, between freedom and necessity, between the individual and the species. Communism is the riddle of history solved, and it knows itself to be this solution. (Karl Marx in Robert C. Tucker, *The Marx-Engels Reader* 1978, 84)

This quote has the typical grandiosity of a genius, but it is also rather German in its teleological or millenarian quality. Yes, big words, but you can Google them. Marx is a smart guy, and he sees through the surface like a laser. But as British economist Joan Robinson said, "The misery of being exploited by capitalists is nothing compared to the misery of not being exploited at all." Also, for some reason, Marx's utopian vision did not include the Gulags and the cultural revolutions of the future. Marx is not bad at looking in the rearview mirror, but his ability to predict the future is pretty awful. A lot of dead people could attest to that, if only they could speak to us from the grave.

I started to talk about motivation in the essay on leadership and management, but I want to add one point about cognitive dissonance. The idea is that sometimes if there is a clash between our ideas and our actions, we will adjust our thinking to reduce the dissonance. In other words, we will rationalize. That is partly why some of us who get paid less for our work get more satisfaction out of it. We tell elaborate tales to ourselves about the importance of what we are doing. Indeed, some people who make a lot of money aren't very happy. I would argue that some of this is simply because they are spoilt rotten, but it is also because they start to get the idea that they are doing their jobs because they have to, not because they want to. Anyway, the takeaway point is that people are complicated psychologically, and because everyone is different and every job is different (even changing from day to day), I just think that placing too much emphasis on deriving our life's meaning from work is foolish. Also, since you might lose your job, it is better not to build your entire sense of self-worth around it.

One final point, we need to mitigate this tendency to play Monday morning quarterback on one another. Of course, the other guy's job always seems easier than yours, but it usually isn't. Also, some of these critics don't know how to do things themselves. Perhaps that is why they are so judgmental. It's easy to criticize. But this modern tendency to make sport out of destroying our fellow Americans suggests that the social fabric is disintegrating. When the boat starts sinking, people go at each other's throats. If we don't see brothership in each other, our country is doomed. It's just that simple.

Finance and Investing

In my book *Basic Stuff That Everyone Should Know*, there is a chapter on finance basics. For you, dear reader, I am going to make it even simpler and higher level.

The financial markets are volatile, and you never really know if the price is right, although you can usually guess when the price is relatively high versus rather low based on historical trends. The past does not necessarily predict the future. Over the very long term, the stock market rises; but over shorter time frames, the market may go up or down or sideways or whatever. So a key decision is whether you are going to be a short-term trader or a long-term investor. You should also diversify into different types of assets because they behave a little differently over time. Studies show that the asset allocation or diversification is the most important element in determining the returns of a portfolio. Just don't overdo it and proliferate investments. Remember the difference between realized and unrealized losses. Even if the market drops, if you haven't sold your stock, nothing whatsoever has happened to you. It's all on paper. Finally, the blatantly obvious: if you don't understand what you are buying, don't buy it.

Professor Connel Fullenkamp has some good DVD courses about finance available from *The Great Courses* collection by the Teaching Company. Also, if you don't have the time to learn about finance, consider a Vanguard index fund. Also bear in mind that financial types are experts at using jargon to dazzle you and cow you into submission. My favorites are *parametric cat bond* and *structured finance*. I have worked in some of the most complex areas of finance, and I can tell you that, like many things, at bottom it is simple.

When I offer to teach people finance basics, some of them say that they don't need to know it because they have no money to invest. Actually, the best thing about investing is that it forces you to take an interest in current events, particularly those that affect the economy. It leads you to a bigger picture view of the world that is much more important than merely filling your pockets with a few extra dollars.

Growing Up in a Farm

My father grew up dirt poor in a plantation in Maui. My best friend at work grew up in a farm in Utah. Talking to them has convinced me that we have lost something in our transition from farming to manufacturing to service, as we have moved from rural to urban, beyond becoming couch potatoes. Here's a list of things you can learn by growing up in a farm:

1. About life and death and disease
2. That life is hard
3. To be God-fearing because your fate depends on things like the weather
4. About business, because farming is a business
5. The value of hard work and getting up early in the morning
6. To care for animals
7. Conservation

8. To love nature and the outdoors
9. The benefits of having numerous children to help you

If we don't learn these things in a farm, how are we going to learn them? That's just a question for our education people to think about.

Here's an example of how our thinking can go wrong when we leave the farm behind. Farmers in some states used to let their cows wander up into the mountains to eat grass in the forest, but in some places, the government made rules to stop this migration to protect the environment. But because the cows weren't eating the grass, the grass grew tall and eventually dried out and produced more wildfires. It is good to remember that the ecosystem has evolved over a very long period of time and that things are the way they are for a reason, even if we puny humans sometimes don't understand it all.

Newton and Payback

Sir Isaac Newton's third law of motion is that for every action, there is an equal and opposite reaction. This is not just true in science but in life. That is why Hinduism and Buddhism have a concept of karma, which means that you pay for your sins. Sooner or later, there is cosmic pushback. A lot of times, it is not cosmic anyway; it is just society pushing back.

When I was younger, I upset people without intending to because I wasn't very empathetic. I think a lot of children are that way, and even though I was not exactly a child in chronological age, I think I was psychologically. But my father was also unempathetic.. I think it is a myth that unempathetic people are not nice people. They can be. They just might not feel sorry for you. Germans have a word called *schaudenfreude*, which means that you take pleasure in the misfortunes of others. That sounds nasty, but if someone has been acting badly and karma sets in on them, a little schaudenfreude is okay in my view—at least up to a point. What goes around comes around, so if you have been hurting people, don't be surprised when you get pushback. You reap what you sow. And if a jerk falls on his face and some of us laugh, too bad.

Elites

I don't believe in elites because they are often self-serving and exploitative. Contrary to what folks like MSNBC anchor Chris Hayes think (see the *Twilight of the Elites*), this is nothing new. Also, in my experience, as Alexis De Tocqueville pointed out in the early 1800s, the best people usually don't seek political office; so we end up with rule by tin gods, puppets, whores, half-wits, and idiot cousins. Well, that's grotesque hyperbole, of course, but I'm pretty angry right now, like a lot of other Americans. In the movie *The American President*, Michael Douglas says, "I was so busy keeping my job that I forgot to do my job." Aaron Sorkin captures in that one line what is wrong with politics today: people who put themselves before their own country.

My mother always taught me about the idea of noblesse oblige. In America, many of us are relatively well-off by comparison to the rest of the world, and our noble values make us into a kind of nobility. So we can all live up to the standard of what an aristocracy is supposed to be. In other words, class is not about money; it is about character and how you were raised. As to the elitism of certain schools, the truth is—and I think by now most Americans realize it—where you go to school isn't really the issue, and anyway, resting on your laurels after going to college is a really stupid thing to do. What you do after school ends is what counts. And by the way, being a snob is not classy. A classy person makes other people feel good about themselves.

I sometimes have this recurring ideation that the best way to restore America is to bomb Harvard. Of course, I don't mean that—at least not completely. But some of these Harvard guys have done real damage to this great country. One of my Columbia professors taught us a joke about these folks: you can always tell a Harvard man, but you can't tell him much. It is a double entendre: either you can't tell him because he knows already or because he is a lunkhead. Stupid people do stupid things, but smart people do also, and it is sometimes because they think they are smarter than they are and that they know more than they do.

Do you know who was the only US president with a PhD? Woodrow Wilson. Very much the theoretician, wouldn't you say? Think about the League of Nations. Do you know who was the only US president with an MBA? George W. Bush, who called himself "the decider" and wrote a book called *Decision Points*—but he also made very shortsighted decisions. Do you like to attack the wrong country? How are those Bush tax cuts working out for you with $19 trillion in debt? I think of our two most important presidents as George Washington and Abraham Lincoln, neither of whom had a college degree or even a lot of formal education. My favorite president of the twentieth century, Ronald Reagan, went to Eureka College, not exactly the Ivy League. Now, this anecdotal evidence isn't proof of much, but it suggests that you don't have to be highly educated to be a good leader.

Communications

The key to communications is knowing that you get out of something what you bring to it. In other words, two people can read the same simple sentence and derive different meanings and interpretations. Someone is talking with a certain intention, but someone is hearing the words, and you don't know exactly how what you say is being perceived. Also, you have to write for many audiences. I once sent a poem to a friend teasing him, but he didn't get the joke, and he sent it to his friends, and they got mad. It just wasn't the kind of thing that would look good in front of a jury or on the front page of a newspaper. So like a lawyer told me once—and it is darn good advice—you write for a lot of audiences, not just the one you intend for the first communication. The other point is that communication is about your brand: everything you say and do sends a message to others about who you are. One of the things I learned early on from people who were more sophisticated than me is that they would do some things not because they wanted to but because of how it made them look. It was a messaging thing.

People say that silence is golden, but I have gotten in trouble for being silent and not disagreeing with someone's bad or erroneous comments. I always thought that people had a right to their opinions because my mother always told me that, but some people think that if you are silent in the face of evil, that is assent. Personally, I don't fight with people over opinions. I will fight them on facts, though, if I can get up the energy.

Because there is a cloud of messages bombarding us every day, it can be hard to get a message through to someone. I have worked on consumer education programs; and a lot of times, they don't work, particularly if the message is complex and if people are not psychologically ready to hear it. Any complex message is likely to be reduced by the listener to a simpler and somewhat inaccurate takeaway. Always remember that words don't resonate unless they ring true. In addition, once you lose your credibility with the audience, you may as well stop talking.

You shouldn't ever say that you agree with someone's point of view or even acknowledge their point of view if you don't know exactly what it is. President Obama once acknowledged the historical grievances of Muslims against the West. So what's the problem with that? There are over a billion Muslims, and who the heck knows how each of them sees their grievances and what they want to do about them?

A careless error for someone trained at the Harvard Law School. That's partly why I write books about the gaps left by our education system. And let us ask ourselves whether overeducation reduces common sense. We should at least think about that. As Yoda says in *The Empire Strikes Back*, following ancient Asian philosophy, sometimes "you must unlearn what you have learned." There is a lot of clutter that can find its way into your head, and you have to cut through it, although it usually takes experience to sort the wheat from the chaff.

Children's Stories

Instead of reading articles by academics, one can profit by reading children's books. We all do it as kids, but then we forget. For example, one of the lessons of "Goldilocks and the Three Bears" is when Goldilocks compares the dishes on the table and the chairs; and one is too big, the other is too small, and the other is just right. This is the golden mean between two extremes advocated by Aristotle in the *Nicomachean Ethics* (and also by Buddha). Or as my mother taught me, "Everything in moderation." I'm not going to say that this is always a good rule, but as an example, it would sure help us rightsize the government.

Another great book is *Chicken Little*, not because it is about being a fraidy cat but because it is about empiricism, and it raises the question of correlation versus causation. Go check things out—was it a piece of the sky or just an apple? Find out for yourself. Don't assume that just because something hit you on the head, it was caused by a falling sky. This is a story about epistemology. Kids don't know that, but you're supposed to as their parents. *The Little Engine That Could* is a story about believing in yourself and not giving up and trying and working hard.

Another excellent book that I didn't learn from as a kid because I could not overcome my insecurities but is a classic is *I'm Tired of Lions*, which is about just being yourself and being happy about that and not comparing yourself to others. Of course, the book isn't completely persuasive because it is never that hard to find out that you're the king of the jungle. But it's a nice message anyway. Finally, although I have no idea whether this book has been condemned as racist, I loved *The Five Chinese Brothers*. This is a book about diversity and teams and how different people bring different strengths to the table. It is about people working together.

Aesop's Fables have a lot of good things in them, albeit some are kind of cryptic. One I like is "The Great and the Little Fishes." The upshot is that big fishes get caught in the net while little ones get away. This is similar to the idea of the ring of power in Plato's *The Republic* (the Ring of Gyges), Wagner's *Ring of the Nibelungs* opera cycle, and Tolkein's *Lord of the Rings*. The ring of power is the ring of invisibility. If you are invisible, there isn't much that you can't have.

Movies

When I was a kid, I wanted to be a movie director. My mother got me a small Bell & Howell Super 8 camera when I was just eleven years old. The cool thing about it was that it had a pinpoint lens that didn't require focusing. See, when you have a genius for a mother, it helps out a lot. Richard Wagner believed that opera was the total artwork or *Gesamtkunstwerk*. In fact, it is movies that bring many different artistic disciplines together in a team effort. I have realized, however, that you cannot have a good movie without a good screenplay. Even some movie experts fail to understand this. James Lipton of the Actors Studio once said that the tragic end of *Million Dollar Baby* showed fearless direction by Clint Eastwood. Uh, the ending was written by the screenwriter. Similarly, some movie historians who like the auteur theory of the director like to find themes running between a director's various movies. Why would there be common themes if the screenwriters were different? Now, maybe a director only picks stories that fit his favorite themes, but I don't know how one can prove that. I still like movies, and I have many favorites, but there are a few that I want to list because I think they have an important message and show that Hollywood is not just about sex and violence, at least not always.

1. *Star Wars*, *The Empire Strikes Back*, and *The Return of the Jedi*. The good-versus-evil and oppressed-versus-tyrant theme is a great one for Americans, but there are also many interesting lines of dialogue in the film. There is also a redemption theme and one of the few examples of the classic Greek drama technique involving the recognition of someone who is in disguise or whom you don't know the true identity of. George Lucas understands politics, and he understands anthropology.
2. *Back to the Future*. This is the cleverest screenplay I ever saw by Bob Zemeckis and Bob Gale. What I like best about the story is that the time-travel aspect suggests that there are moments in everyone's life where choices are made and which determine the course of the future.
3. *It's a Wonderful Life*. This film is a bit sappy, but there is great truth to the idea that if we are not born, we do not know what the loss can be. I look back on my life, and it is clear that this is true. Some people call it the ripple effect.

4. *Superman.* Great direction by Richard Donner, whom you can sort of tell started out doing television commercials. Fine story by Mario Puzo and beautiful cinematography of the American Midwest by British photographer Geoffrey Unsworth (he also did *2001: A Space Odyssey*). Three times Lois Lane is supposed to die a horrible death, and three times Superman saves her. Good love story, that.
5. *The Electric Horseman.* This Sidney Pollack film is about not allowing yourself to be corrupted by the system. Plus, it has nice pictures of the West.
6. *To Kill a Mockingbird.* This film is usually known as a pro-civil rights movie, but it is more important as a movie about a single father raising two children. Gregory Peck is my favorite actor, so I am biased, but I would say this was the greatest performance by a lead actor in movie history. Peck went to Berkeley, and he was no dummy.
7. *The Omen.* Stephen King said this film was silly, and there are elements of that in it. Billy Graham said that he could not believe Gregory Peck had done a film about the destruction of the family. In fact, Peck got the role because Dick Van Dyke had turned down the part because he thought the movie was gory. But the film is beautiful because it is the story of a strong man who is brought down by his

Achilles' heel, which is his abiding love for his wife. Most people don't see the film as a romance, but it is one of the great ones.

8. *Spartacus*. I like Kirk Douglas because he was the kind of tough guy that my father was, but also because director Stanley Kubrick was a childhood hero of mine. This film shows good versus evil and the depravity, vanity, and love of power of some people. I actually think it is better than *Lawrence of Arabia*. A very underrated movie.
9. *The American President*. Very clever screenplay by the great Aaron Sorkin with some wonderful, pithy statements about government that I can confirm are on target. Good introduction to politics for those who don't like politics. I never thought I would see Michael Douglas, Martin Sheen, and Michael Fox together because they have something in common as actors, although I couldn't put my finger on exactly what. As an aside, I also thought I would never see William Shatner and Christopher Plummer together due to certain similarities between them, but they were together in *Star Trek VI: the Undiscovered Country*.
10. *The Manchurian Candidate* (original 1962 version in black and white). Based on Richard Condon's book, there is an element of social and political satire

in this film that makes it more than an ordinary thriller. A great performance by Angela Lansbury in a part that destroys gender stereotypes (or does it?). It has the funniest line ever in American film history when Lawrence Harvey says, "Twelve days of Christmas? One day is loathsome enough." The meritorious theme? That courage is sometimes found where you least expect it.

11. *Chariots of Fire*. Good film, maybe not great, but a nice take on the workings of God and religion in the world. Whether God is really that interventionist, I don't know, but as someone once told me, God works through us.
12. *The Right Stuff*. I hated all docudramas until I saw this masterwork by Philip Kaufman. Anyone who doubts the greatness and exceptionalism of Americans should watch this movie. Although I admit, it is maybe more for guys than girls.
13. *Bull Durham*. This film isn't one of the best, but it is notable as a story about life not being very fair and about how not everyone gets to be number one and you just have to accept it because that's life. I think a lot of people can relate to that.
14. *Excalibur*. A retelling of the Arthurian legend by the great director John Boorman. Far more realistic than *Camelot* but notable for the depiction

of a husband who remains dedicated to his wife despite her betrayal. Also, an amazing performance by Nigel Terry as Arthur goes from a young boy to an old man. For those who find that they like John Boorman, they might want to watch a largely unknown comedy called *Where the Heart Is*. It might seem like a romp and a frolic, but a lot of deep thinking and artistry went into it. A real gem.

15. *The Elephant Man*. Still David Lynch's best film because it is the least weird, and I like black and white anyway. Nice story about a very unfortunate man who maintained his faith in God. Also a nice look at how people use one another and even sometimes don't know they are doing it. Pretty realistic.

16. *The Wind and the Lion*. John Milius's masterpiece, and kind of quaint given our current relations with certain terrorists from that part of the world. But I always liked love stories where the lovers don't have sex or even kiss. *The Remains of the Day* is like that, and that is a fine movie, but *The Wind and the Lion* is faster paced.

17. *Sleeping Beauty*. Great Disney animation, and the story about a woman's vanity and the destruction it causes is still fun for me, even if some people think it is sexist. Actually, men have vanity also, and sometimes far worse. Mirror, mirror on the

wall, who's the fairest of them all? I love that. Not that I don't spend more than $10 for a haircut, you understand.

18. *Quiz Show*. A gem by director Robert Redford that has a nice supporting performance by the great director Martin Scorsese. This film raises the question about why honesty matters and why even a little lie can lead you down a slippery slope. It also raises the question about why growing up privileged can be a problem.
19. *Miller's Crossing*. Brilliant screenplay and direction by the Cohen brothers. I like this film because it shows a guy who is just darn smart maneuvering around people who aren't nearly as smart as he is.
20. *Videodrome*. I really hesitate to put this on the list. Some might see this film as one for sickos and perverts, and it is surely rated R. The reason I like it is because it is very original, and it took massive courage for David Cronenberg to write it and direct it. Even today, I feel that I take a risk by endorsing it. You might hate the film, but I give Cronenberg credit.
21. *The Great Santini*. Nice story about a military family. Some civil rights stuff in there. Notable mostly for a stunningly beautiful performance by Blythe Danner as a strong and dedicated Southern military wife.

Although this is just a movie, I believe there are women like that.

22. *Smilla's Sense of Snow*. Great story by Peter Hoeg with maybe the greatest part for a lead actress I have ever seen. Plus, the cinematographer obviously loved Julia Ormond. She never looked better (had the right haircut), and she gives a strong performance, which was nominated for an Academy Award.

It is kind of bad that I didn't include any films by my favorite directors Steven Spielberg and Martin Scorsese, but again, the movie starts with the screenplay. It is also kind of bad that I have no Audrey Hepburn films on the list. I love Audrey Hepburn. When they made her, they broke the mold. You could see her emotions floating across her face, especially in her eyes. Incredible actress and one of the great beauties.

Books

It can be hard to decide what to read. People don't have the time, money, or desire to read everything in sight. So let me just make a couple of key recommendations in order to save the reader some trouble.

1. The US Constitution (original text) and *Essential Supreme Court Decisions* by John R. Vile. If you don't know how our government works, it is hard to affect the future of your country. Two separate books are being recommended here. If you don't want to read the entire Constitution, you can just read the Bill of Rights.
2. *Modern Times* by Paul Johnson. This is a history of the twentieth century by a conservative, prowhite people historian. That part you might not like, depending on who you are; but he tells the truth about the failure of communism and social engineering, which people should know so we don't do the same foolish stuff again and again.

3. *The Economic Transformation of America: 1600 to the Present* by Robert Heilbroner and Aaron Singer. Short and simply written. If business leaves you cold, try Eric Foner's book *The Story of American Freedom.*
4. *How the Economy Works: Confidence, Crashes and Self-Fulfilling Prophecies* by Roger E. A. Farmer. It is very difficult to find a good one-volume book of economics. I have a shelf full of economics books, and you learn a bit here and there from all them. But Farmer's book is about the best if you are interested in macroeconomic policy and can only read one book. His policy solution seems strange to me, but his exposition of the past is terrific.
5. *The History of Western Philosophy* by Bertrand Russell. To read philosophy, you sort of have to read the original text, but not many have the time for that, and many of these ideas are outdated. The reason for knowing this material is that it can give you a sense of how ideas developed in Western history and how some of them are still clanking around in people's heads today. Thus, if you are not going to read original text, then the Russell book is good because he not only describes the philosophy but also the history. This book is not for everyone, but it is a good book for the right person. Now, if you want to try to read a philosophy book in the original text,

try Plato's *The Republic*. It is part philosophy, part fiction and pretty wild.

6. *A Whack on the Side of the Head* by Roger von Oech. This is a book about creativity. Now, I'm not sure you can really teach creativity. But this is still an important book for managers, particularly if they aren't creative themselves. I think this is a good book for high school students.
7. *Oresteia* by Aeschylus. Everyone should read some Greek tragedy because they understood the human condition well, and Aeschylus is more beautiful poetically than Sophocles or Euripides. We usually teach *Oedipus Rex* in high school. Now, answer me this: what is so tragic about a guy who kills his father in order to sleep with his mother? Do you feel sorry for him? That guy is a creep.
8. *Hamlet: The Prince of Denmark* by William Shakespeare. The greatest play by the greatest writer in history. I could talk about this play for an hour, so I won't even try in this small space. If there is a more difficult role for an actor, I don't know what it is. This is because Hamlet wears masks for the various people in his kingdom, so he is acting various roles himself inside the play. Pretty darn complex. This is a revenge tragedy, a play about karma and what happens when the Christian order is violated by human arrogance

and evil. Actually, some people misunderstand the play. Hamlet is not indecisive. He knows from the get-go what he has to do. He says, "Oh, cursèd sprite that ever I was born to set things right." He is waiting for the right moment to act. Forget about that "To be or not to be" thing. That's not the only line in the play. Come on, you English teachers. You can't teach reading if you can't do it yourself.

9. *Tono-Bungay* by H. G. Wells. Wells is a great writer and a genius, more than most people know. This book has humor, a send-up of the ruling class, a story about business boom and bust, a little weirdness about radioactivity and its analogy to a decaying society. And what I like the best about the story—an impossible love blocked by class. This thing has everything! Well, everything that I like, that is.

10. "Sonnet 138" by Shakespeare. "When my love swears that she is made of truth." This is not a book, just a short poem; but the notable use of legal rhetoric and the depth of the insight into human psychology is staggering. If you read nothing else by Shakespeare, read this sonnet. It proves that intelligence is a relative thing.

11. "Frost at Midnight" by Samuel Taylor Coleridge. Again, a poem, not a book, and you can Google it.

This is just damn good writing. We don't know how to do this anymore. I'm not exactly sure why.

12. *The Haunting of Hill House* by Shirley Jackson. People go on endlessly about the simple prose of Ernest Hemmingway. I take nothing away from him, but to me, Shirley Jackson writes better. Here, she scares the reader by creating an ambiguity between reality, psychology, and the supernatural. How she did that is anybody's guess, but it ain't easy to do, let me tell you. She makes it look easy.
13. I want to recommend two short stories: "Winter Dreams" by F. Scott Fitzgerald and "The Innocent" by Graham Greene. Both are short and deal with impossible romances, one of my favorite story lines.

There are a lot of other good books, some of which are cited here and there in this book. You don't always find the truth in a book, but it is a way of getting outside your own experience and learning from others.

Music

I'm a classical music nut, with a particular affinity for German music. I play the piano, and I think I have reasonable instincts about the German spirit. I was going to list a lot of pieces and show you around the tradition, but I changed my mind about the approach. What I recommend is that you get a sampler box set of top classical pieces such as the one by the London Philharmonic or the collection by Deutsche Grammophon. Start there, live with it awhile, because classical music takes some getting used to. After that, you can probe around on Spotify, Pandora, or YouTube. Part of the fun of this genre is in the discovery, and I don't want to spoil that by being too directive.

Anyway, there is some subjectivity in music tastes as you already know. As to symphonies, my favorite has always been the Mahler Fourth Symphony. As to solo piano music, try the Schubert Piano Sonata in A major D. 664 (opus 120). As to piano concertos, try the Grieg Piano Concerto in A to start with. As to violin concertos, try the Mendelssohn

Violin Concerto in E minor. Now, if you think it is easy to pick one thing out like that from a whole tradition, it isn't. Not everyone could do it. Some music lovers like everything, and they just can't make up their minds. To discern subtle differences takes significant experience. Try to remember that what you hear in classical music on day one is not the same as what you hear after forty years of listening. Finally, while classical music might have been snobby in the past, modern technology makes it something that anyone can enjoy, not just someone with extra money to spend.

Recommending classical music performers is very tricky because there is a lot of subjectivity involved. I can't say definitively that so and so is the best performer. I can only say whom I personally like based on my own preferences. My favorite pianists are Maurizio Pollini, Lang Lang, Vladimir Ashkenazy, and—when it comes to Bach—András Schiff. My favorite conductors are Herbert von Karajan, Otto Klemperer, Carlo Maria Giulini, Adrian Boult, Rafael Kubelík, Carlos Kleiber, Christoph von Dohnányi, Pierre Monteux, and Charles Dutoit. That list would get me into a fistfight with most any music aficionado, but—as the emperor says in the movie *Amadeus*—there it is. By the way, when watching *Amadeus*, the original cut is better than the longer director's cut. The same thing was true of *Close Encounters of the Third Kind*. My advice is that when you either win an Academy Award or are nominated, resist the temptation to "fix" the movie afterward.

As to popular music, I have been working hard to learn it over the last few years, and therefore I am no expert. So again, instead of a long list, I'm going to just give one recommendation for each genre to get you started—although, no doubt, most of you are further ahead than me.

1. Jazz. The jazz version of Gershwin's *Porgy and Bess* by Louis Armstrong and Ella Fitzgerald.
2. Pop or soft rock. Blondie's *Greatest Hits*. I may get laughed at for this (although it won't be the first time, let me tell you). Not all these songs are great, but the great ones are very snappy.
3. Hard rock. Guns N' Roses's *Appetite for Destruction*. Quick-paced energy.
4. Country. "Sweet Dreams" sung by Patsy Cline (or perhaps "The Tennessee Waltz" sung by Patti Page).
5. Soul. "Will You Love Me Tomorrow" sung by The Shirelles.
6. Traditional. Toss-up between "Auld Lang Syne" and "America, the Beautiful."
7. Solo female vocal. Doris Day's *The Christmas Album*. I have defended Doris Day against many people who think she is stupid and that I am fruity. Actually, she is greatness personified if you like sound quality and the precision control of phrasing. I am faithful to Day, but one other singer who turned my head

was Sarah McLachlan in *The Classic Christmas Album*. Not all the songs are great, but she is quite the songbird.

8. Solo male vocal. David Bowie's *Best of Bowie*. This man is a genius with a distinctive voice and a real sense for business and fashion. He also has an unusual sense of beat, which I call the Bowie head fake. You'll see. A cool music video with Bowie is "Let's Dance." It's very simple but direct and powerful.
9. Movie music. Hard to pick from a lot of great stuff, but have you heard the main title theme from the James Bond film *You Only Live Twice* by John Barry? His mother was a pianist, and his father was a film projectionist. Destiny at work. For those astrology lovers out there, he was a Scorpio, and those intense emotions are displayed very directly. His ability to create nice melodies rivals Tchaikovsky and Chopin.
10. Greatest song ever. "Begin the Beguine" by Cole Porter. I have the John Williams/Boston Pops, the Artie Shaw Orchestra, and the Broadway version from *Jubilee*. I don't know if any of them gets all the way there to what is possible. Also note that they did a vocal version with a pretty blonde lady singing in the movie *The Rocketeer*. If that doesn't sell you, men, then you are a cold fish indeed. I couldn't exactly say

why I think this is the greatest song, and certainly Dave Grusin deserves an honorable mention for "It Might Be You" from *Tootsie*, as does Frederick Loewe for "If Ever I Would Leave You" from *Camelot*. But Porter's piece is shaped well, and it builds beautifully and is powered by a slightly syncopated beat underneath. Powerful cumulative effect.

Miscellaneous Rantings

In this essay, I will rant about various topics that I can't fit into a larger topic area and in no particular order.

One of B. F. Skinner's most important insights in his book *Beyond Freedom and Dignity* is that if you want to change yourself, you need to put yourself in a new environment and let it work on you. I don't think that is the only way you can change because you can change by doing new things and also by asking God for some help in a sincere way, but it is a smart comment. In fact, one of the reasons I went to New York City for college is because I thought that, as a guy who grew up in Hawaii and spent almost every weekend on a beach on the North Shore of Oahu, I might need the operant conditioning.

Bashing government can be fun, but like all fun things, you may pay a price for doing it. As confidence erodes in government (and other institutions), it may become harder to recruit people for those jobs in the future, and that is only going to make matters worse. There could be a snowballing effect. It is a myth that government workers are stupid. I have worked in government a long time. Do I sound stupid to you? Most government jobs require a college degree and some prior private sector experience. It's not just a feeder from the local insane asylum like some people think.

The profit motive can be contrary to good information-sharing practices. If people can gain power and money by hoarding information, and if access to information is limited to those with money, then we may create dysfunction for ourselves. I'm not sure this is completely fixable, nor perhaps should it be fixed if services are the basis for the economy, but we just need to be aware of the issue. Also, the Internet is helpful in being largely a free system. This book in your hands didn't cost you that much relative to the value of the information inside it, did it? That is because the impact of information is directly proportional to the scope of its dispersion. Wow, nice aphorism, if I say so myself.

We are looking into computer devices more and more, but we always need to ask ourselves if the world is inside a computer. I once told a high procurement officer in the government that it would be better if we could go out and talk to our business contacts in order to locate good vendors by word of mouth. She said, "We don't have a database like that." I said, "It's not in a database. You have to talk to people." We just need to remember that the world out there is not completely represented inside the machines in our offices and homes. In addition, there is the question of the reliability of the information and data we have on our machines.

I'm a bit worried about Siri and Echo answering questions. Where are those answers coming from? How can we validate them? You can see how a totalitarian person with an Echo in everyone's home could exert incredible power and control over the public. Watch out for that one. Coming soon to a theater near you. We all know about the effect that computers and the Internet are having on killing jobs and brick-and-mortar businesses. Just something to keep an eye on. Maybe one day we can, like Captain Picard says in *Star Trek: First Contact*, just work to better ourselves and not for money.

Technology can make the system more fragile and difficult to fix. Also, while some nerds want to compile giant databases and mine them, we do not always need to do that to come up with solutions. If we want to fight obesity, tell people to drink water and not sugary drinks. There, no data. Knowing a lot about a problem doesn't mean that you are going to solve it because there is often opposition to change. Finally, we need to be in charge of technology and not let it be in charge of us. Letting IT geeks run the world is almost as dumb as letting lawyers run the world. For a long time, humanity got along fine without computers, and we should remember that the world didn't come to an end.

Albert Einstein is purported to have said that the definition of insanity is doing the same thing over and over again and expecting a different result. Point of order: even if you do something different, that doesn't mean that is going to work either. Therefore, this argument isn't worth much in and of itself.

There is a tension between short-term and long-term thinking. We have to get through today in order to get to tomorrow. But merely thinking ahead to the next election or the next shareholder report isn't a good idea either. I think good leaders do think long-term. It's just that they are often too busy putting out fires, reading e-mails, and sitting in stupid meetings to do anything about it. I never liked John Maynard Keynes's view that "in the long run, we are all dead" because it doesn't make for good policy.

If we think about organizational change, we need to think about whether it occurs from the top down or from the bottom up. To me, most ideas need to come from the bottom up, but change must be directed from the top down. Implementation requires buy-in from the top and the bottom (and the middle, for that matter). Anytime that we try to make changes, there is resistance, but that is just human nature, and it can come from a CEO as easily as a janitor.

In a world of reality-television stars, selfies, and sexting—we need to ask ourselves whether we find meaning in the greater glory of God and in helping our fellow man, or whether we find it in the applause of others. A little of both, perhaps, and again, the golden mean makes sense: everything in moderation, don't go to extremes.

We do need to think about the difference between cultures and not simply say that inside of every fill-in-the-blank foreigner, there is an American just waiting to get out. For example, when John Kerry took James Taylor to France to sing "You've Got a Friend" to a bunch of French diplomats, did he think about how that video would play with our Arab and Persian extremist enemies in the Middle East or with Vladimir Putin? To them, it was probably the equivalent of wearing a pink tutu and dancing around. It's not only embarrassing to do something like that; it's dangerous.

A pet peeve I have is when people react before they are done listening. I have often had people talk over me before I am done speaking. As someone said once, you learn a lot more by listening than speaking. Listen first, think, then react. Or get ready to be called stupid and arrogant behind your back and all over town. Try not to embarrass your parents. Try.

Another pet peeve that I have is when I see people driving or walking while looking into their electronic devices. Adults used to admonish us when we were young: "Hey, kid, look where you're going." This is also a philosophical issue. It is better to spend more time looking into the front-view window of your car than in the rearview mirror. Holding on to the past and nursing grudges isn't always a good idea. The past does not exist. The future may never come. One of my favorite moments in movies is from *Meatballs* when Bill Murray says, "It just doesn't matter, it just doesn't matter, it just doesn't matter." That is exactly what my mother used to teach me: "Nothing matters." But at same time, please realize that if you have done someone wrong and they die, then you have a karmic problem. You have to act as if you and those you love may die tomorrow because in the odd case, that's what can happen.

Finally, we must think about *is* versus *ought*. Is the glass half empty or is the glass half full? Can people change? Can society change? Can we reach utopia? Truly, some improvement is possible, but not total improvement. There are limits. Social engineering has failed, but I think that we can continue to improve incrementally through the free exchange of ideas and a relatively free market system. As we do this, however, we must remain realistic. We may not have to accept the world as it is, but we must take it as we find it. You can't get to utopia by living in a dream world.

Western History

In the movie *RoboCop*, the media teaser is, "You give us three minutes. We'll give you the world." That was intended as a joke, but in fact, we see even shorter segments on cable television today taking the viewer on a whirlwind tour of current events. I'm going to try something even crazier. I'm going to try to describe the whole arc of Western history in about the same three minutes from *RoboCop*. The reason is simply that it is too easy, when reading a five-hundred- or one-thousand-page history book, to lose the forest for the trees.

A big part of history involves the development of technology and its effect on human society. This life of the nomadic hunter changed when people started to live in small villages, and it changed again when it became possible for large numbers of people to live together in urban areas supported by food brought in from a distance. These kinds of changes are enabled by technology. Think about the major shifts that occurred with the domestication of plants and animals, irrigation, metallurgy, writing, paper, money, the bow and arrow, the gun, the printing press, the steam engine, the flush toilet, the car, the airplane, the lightbulb, the telegraph, the telephone, the refrigerator, the washing machine, the computer, the graphical interface, the spreadsheet, the Internet, the cell phone—to name a few. Each of these inventions revolutionized human life and the way we interact. As these changes took hold, we shifted from a largely agrarian economy, where people were generally poor and had shorter life spans, to one based more on manufacturing, where some people had a chance to get richer and people needed to migrate to urban areas. The history of economic development is the history of technological innovation, but as Paul Johnson has observed in his book *Enemies of Society*, innovation requires freedom, which in turn requires the right kind of political and social structure. That is why the rate of innovation and change differs between countries over time.

The big change was the Industrial Revolution, but industrialization continues today. In the mid-twentieth century, developed economies began shifting more toward services and away from manufacturing. Many nations of the world that were once considered poor are now competing with the United States. Better transportation systems mean that the world is a small place and that the economies of various countries are interlinked to a greater extent than before. The spread of the market system has helped to move more people out of poverty and has supported population increases and environmental degradation. The market system's ability to give people the benefits of applied science, sometimes called *technology*, has increased faith in science and deemphasized religion.

Politically, the world has shifted from local tribal governance toward increasingly centralized control across wider geographic areas. We have seen the rise of the modern bureaucracy, which is necessary to maintain control and provide services. Autocracy has often been replaced by democracy, although not everywhere; and there is increasing recognition of individual rights, but to varying degrees. The severe kind of central planning and social engineering of Communism was discredited by the events of the twentieth century, and most countries today are a mixed bag of government and markets. After World War II, the United States and its allies erected a system of international law, and today a few even dream of a world governance structure.

Demographically, European colonization of non-Western countries was only part of a larger continuing trend toward migration of people to new lands. More diversity has resulted. While some races and cultures have been assimilated into others, some groups have been unable to assimilate, thereby creating conflict.

Henry Kissinger wrote a concise summation of the development of ideas:

> Every age has its leitmotif, a set of beliefs that explains the universe, that inspires or consoles the individual by providing an explanation for the multiplicity of events impinging on him. In the medieval period, it was religion; in the Enlightenment, it was Reason; in the nineteenth and twentieth centuries, it was nationalism combined with a view of history as a motivating force. Science and technology are the governing concepts of our age" (*World Order* 2014, 330)

In that larger scheme, there were a couple of pivotal events:

1. Discovery that the earth revolved around the sun and that the stars weren't fixed in the firmament around the earth
2. Martin Luther and the Protestant Reformation
3. Charles Darwin's theory of evolution or natural selection
4. Dating of the age of the earth and the universe

These events exacerbated the conflict between religion and science.

Also, just to focus in on a specific example for illustrative purposes, the Christianity of the medieval Catholic Church was not the same as that of, say, Joel Osteen. Back in the old days, if you were a peasant and got punched out by a knight, the priest would say, "Tough, just be happy eating your squirrel and get back to work." Joel Osteen (among others) sometimes tells people that God wants them to get a better job or be rich. Now, putting aside the question of whether Osteen is pushing a cotton-candy form of Christianity and what this has to do with the book of Job, we can see that there has been a big change that reflects the underlying changes in the world we live in.

Now, a few words about the writing of history are in order.

Strangely, the best statement I have seen on the question of whether history repeats itself is not by a historian but by a famous German conductor named Wilhelm Furtwängler. In 1948, he said,

> But since historical situations never literally repeat themselves, analogies are invariably false, no matter how compelling they may appear at first sight. (*Concerning Music*, 1977, 69)

This idea has concurrence from historian Mark A. Stoler in his audio course *The Skeptic's Guide to American History*. It is also concurred to by Nassim Nicholas Taleb, who said, "The inability to predict outliers implies the inability to predict the course of history, given the share of these events in the dynamics of events" (*The Black Swan* 2010, xxiv).

I will also note the dangers of the "pastoral" or the tendency for some people to look back fondly on a past history that never actually happened. We can see that in the longing people have for the 1950s and 1960s in America.

One problem with this view is that it was probably better to be white and male then than black or female. The other problem with this view is that "Europe was flat on its back amid its own rubble. Asia was a rice paddy" (Glenn Hubbard and Peter Navarro, *Seeds of Destruction* 2011, xiii). You can see the pastoral in people who long for the days before capitalism took hold. Yes, there were no stinky carbon-spewing smokestacks. But there was also no running water, no flush toilets, no central heating, no refrigerators—and if a rich guy wanted to hurt you, he could. You get the idea. Don't long for a past that never was.

Some people have tried to find larger trends in history. For example, some people think that as capitalism takes hold, you get more democracy. Others think that as technology improves, you get more democracy. Others think that as democracy spreads, you get more stability, more prosperity, and less war. I'm not sure that any of these theories holds up to scrutiny. There are too many exceptions to the rule to establish a rule. George W. Bush and Paul Wolfowitz thought it would be fairly easy to establish a democracy and market system in Iraq. Actually, it is not easy to do that because the institutions that support both are hard to develop and cultures differ. We make a big mistake trying to make others over in our own image.

In addition, any rule that is not predictive isn't very useful. I recall reading a long history book by Paul Kennedy, the chair of the Yale history department, called *The Rise and Fall of the Great Powers*. Kennedy had derived various megatrends from world history. So what's the problem with that? Shortly after the book came out, the Soviet Union collapsed, something Kennedy apparently had no idea would happen. So much for trend analysis, huh?

Finally, it is important to realize that history is cherry-picked fact, and it reflects certain biases of the author. That is why you get a different feel about America from reading Howard Zinn's *A People's History of the United States* than when you read Paul Johnson's *A History of the American People*. History is not fiction, but it is not science either. Also—and this is blatantly obvious—most things that happen in the world never get reported in a periodical, let alone a history book.

To a Christian, while humans may not understand history, there is a larger plan that God is pursuing. I have no idea how an atheist can stand the anxiety associated with the idea that all is randomness and the vagaries of Fortune. Perhaps, as Forest Gump says, "Maybe it's both, both happening at the same time." I don't really know.

Looking Forward

I'm not a futurist, but when I look ahead, some of what I see coming doesn't look very good to me. I think we need to get on the stick. First, we need to deal with our fiscal problems at the federal government level; and to do that, we have to beat back this tendency of baby boomers to be selfish. Second, we need to avoid getting in the way of family formation and the desire of many couples to have children. As we all know, the family is the foundation for society. Third, we need to improve education K-12 and find a way to reduce the costs of higher education without damaging our academic research and scholarship. Fourth, we have to take people as individuals and not paint with a broad brush using stereotypes. In this regard, we should stop calling people *racist* and just call them *biased* so they might be willing to admit it at the same time that we acknowledge that you cannot completely remove biases from human beings. Fifth, we need to understand that the world is outside our homes, offices, and computer devices.

Sixth, we need to recognize that we are all in the same boat and try to work together. Seventh, we need to be realistic about the fact that security and the rule of the law form the foundation for our society and our economy. Eighth, we need to stop lying and get away from this idea that the ends justify the means. Ninth, we need to be grateful for small things and count our blessings. Tenth, we need to follow the Golden Rule.

Push the easy button, right? We know what we need to do. We just need the will to do it.

Afterword

Most major religions and philosophers thought that helping others and civic duty matter. My view is that that this is true only if you know what you're doing. Busybody, goody-two-shoes people can be a menace if they try to fix things that they don't know how to fix. For my own part, I'm altruistic, but for purely selfish reasons. We're all in the same boat, so if I am helping my community and country, the main reason could be just that I am trying to protect my investments. Altruism can be the height of selfishness. In my view, you can't get rich unless you help people. You can't make new friends without making a gesture and doing a small favor here and there. You can't be thought well of unless you try to pay back those who helped you in the past if you ever get the chance. You can't become important unless you make others feel important. But at the same time, you have to be potentially dangerous. People have to know that if they take an unwarranted, unprovoked shot at you, they might pay a price—maybe not today, maybe not tomorrow, but someday, and for the rest of their lives.

Sometimes we overcomplicate things. If you want to be respected, be respectable. If you want to have credibility, then be right. If you want to have friends, then don't be a jerk. If you go around pushing people, then expect pushback. If you want to learn things, then be willing to listen and find out more. I can summarize these few points even more simply: try to have a little class and don't think that the world revolves around you.

Now, I don't know if these thoughts are particularly Christian, and I'm sure that some people would say that I've been an inferior Christian anyway. These are just my personal observations about life.

If I had to put the purpose of this book into a nutshell, it would be this: to help to correct the economics problem of asymmetric information. I think that redistributing income is a rather clumsy way of solving economic inequalities. The more elegant solution is redistributing information. But clearly, I can't do it alone. This will require a team effort. And I don't mean that you have to stand in a classroom, although that is a noble endeavor. You could do it over lunch, or an e-mail, or by way of a phone call, or by wandering over to the next cubicle and having a chat.

When I was in law school, I read an article in *Scientific American* about how if you are in a poor, undeveloped country, it makes no sense to build an expensive hospital with current technology. What makes more sense is giving everyone an immunization shot and thereby bring the health of the many up a little bit. This book is based on the same premise: we need to raise consciousness about how we think about the world a little bit across the board if we want to improve things.

My hope is that this book has a perennial quality and is not just a flash in the pan. Ecclesiastes 1:10 says, "Is there any thing whereof it may be said, See, this is new? It hath been already of old time, which was before us." Now, we know that technology changes a lot over time, and this has huge effects; so in that regard, Ecclesiastes is not right. But I think he is talking more about human nature and the things that people do. In that regard, I suggest that we have not changed that much since the time of Ecclesiastes. Because of that, books that talk truthfully about what it is to be human should have lasting value.

The most important thing to remember is that people are not perfect, and they are never going to be, so they cannot be held to that standard. That is why the Bible says, "Judge not that ye be not judged." But I actually prefer Shakespeare's version of this idea from *Henry IV* when he says, "Banish plump Jack, and banish all the world." He is talking about Jack Falstaff, a likeable fat buffoon. Shakespeare knew that people were mediocrities because he was a genius among geniuses, but he didn't feel the need to put others down in order to make himself feel superior. Shakespeare accepted people for what they were. There is an important lesson in that.

Finally, people sometimes ask me how I can pull off a writing project while having a full-time job. I have to make a space in the time outside the office. A good statement of what is required is from William Deresiewicz, who writes,

> The ability to engage in introspection, I suggested, is the essential precondition for living the life of the mind, and the essential precondition for introspection is solitude. (*Excellent Sheep: the Miseducation of the American Elite and the Way to a Meaningful Life* 2014, 2)

That, and you need some disposable income so that you can buy books and other information.

I hope I have provided good value for the price. Thanks for picking up my book and taking the time to read it.